THE REFERENCE SHELF   VOLUME 36 NUMBER 1

AMERICAN CULTURE IN THE SIXTIES

EDITED BY VINETA COLBY

THE H. W. WILSON COMPANY
NEW YORK   1964

THE REFERENCE SHELF

The books in this series reprint articles, excerpts from books, and addresses on current issues, social trends, and other aspects of American life, and occasional surveys of foreign countries. There are six separately bound numbers in each volume, all of which are generally published in the same calendar year. One number is a collection of recent speeches on a variety of subjects; each of the remaining numbers is devoted to a single subject and gives background information and discussion from varying points of view, followed by a comprehensive bibliography.

Subscribers to the current volume receive the books as issued. The subscription rate is $12 ($15 foreign) for a volume of six numbers. The price of single numbers is $3 each.

PREFACE

It is the purpose of this compilation to survey the phenomenon of American culture in the sixties and to attempt to single out for closer scrutiny and evaluation some of the specific areas of its development—art, literature, theatre, music, ballet, and the mass media of motion pictures and television. Such material as has been collected here is merely a fraction of the enormous amount of recent writing on the subject. The bibliography, while selective and necessarily limited in scope, will nevertheless give the reader some inkling of the range and variety of material which is readily available.

The editor is indebted to the authors and publishers who have granted permission to reprint their work and to the staff of the Paul Klapper Library of Queens College, the City University of New York, for cooperation and innumerable courtesies.

VINETA COLBY

January 1964

PREFACE

CONTENTS

I. AMERICAN CULTURE: AS OTHERS SEE US

EDITOR'S INTRODUCTION

In 1835 a visiting Frenchman reporting on his travels concluded sympathetically but regretfully that for all its virtues America was culturally barren. Culture, Alexis de Tocqueville suggested, was a luxury which a growing democracy could not afford:

It would be to waste the time of my readers and my own, if I strove to demonstrate how the general mediocrity of fortunes, the absence of superfluous wealth, the universal desire for comfort, and the constant efforts by which everyone attempts to procure it, make the taste for the useful predominate over the love of the beautiful in the heart of man. Democratic nations, among whom all these things exist, will therefore cultivate the arts which serve to render life easy, in preference to those whose object is to adorn it. They will habitually prefer the useful to the beautiful, and they will require that the beautiful should be useful.

In 1962 another visiting Frenchman, André Malraux, French Minister of State for Cultural Affairs, toasted the United States as "a citadel of culture":

For culture, for an Atlantic civilization, for the freedom of the mind, I offer a toast to the only nation that has waged war but not worshipped it, that has won the greatest power in the world but not sought it, that has wrought the greatest weapon of death but not wished to wield it; and may it inspire men with dreams worthy of its action.

Thus within the span of a little less than a century and a half, American culture has come a long way. Many foreign visitors once mocked or deplored America's cultural wasteland—Mrs. Frances Trollope, Charles Dickens, Matthew Arnold. Many Americans—Henry James, James McNeill Whistler, Gertrude Stein, T. S. Eliot, Ernest Hemingway—fled their country to the more culturally stimulating atmosphere of England and the Continent. Some, like H. L. Mencken, remained at home but

7

grumbled bitterly about the "booboisie," the absence of an intellectual aristocracy, the powerful "mass" society which Mencken described as "more capable of putting its idiotic ideas into execution than anywhere else," and the ruling plutocracy—"ignorant, hostile to inquiry, tyrannical in the exercise of its power, suspicious of ideas of whatever sort."

American culture still has its critics—more impassioned and articulate than ever perhaps, certainly better fortified with scientifically gathered data. But today it also has its defenders. Significantly, these are not merely chauvinistic boosters who believe that American culture is best simply because it is American. On the contrary, these defenders are as articulate and as well armed with documentary evidence as the detractors. Indeed, their evidence is overwhelming. The data and statistics demonstrate beyond all question that American culture in the sixties is burgeoning as at no other time in this country's history.

"Cultural boom" and "cultural explosion" are perhaps unhappy phrases for describing this phenomenon, carrying as they do connotations of destruction and fragmentation. Nevertheless they are apt metaphors. American culture in the sixties is not the offspring of a long, leisurely evolution, but of a jet-propelled, sky-rocketing, outer-space orbiting age. It is also the offspring of subtle economic, political, social, and psychological influences. The explosion, if we must call it that, has taken place in the 1960's because America has at last settled down after the unsettling experiences of World War II, which established this country once and for all as a major international power. Our provincialism, our isolationism, our ignorance of foreign lands and cultures have all but vanished. As our minds and intellectual horizons broaden, the world shrinks in size. A journey of a few hours by air brings us to any part of the world. A flick of the television dial does almost the same.

It is disquieting to reflect that our cultural explosion followed swiftly upon the literal explosions of A-bombs and the threat of super-bombs. If there is a connection here, it is tenuous and probably has something to do with our sense of urgency, our need to find meaning and values in life. But the more obvious fuse that set off our cultural explosion is economic—a thriving postwar economy, employment, job security, labor-saving devices and leisure. Culture clings to the tail of the inflationary spiral, thereby demonstrating the correctness of De Tocqueville's view that it *is* a luxury. In the 1960's we can afford it. We can afford the education—schools, colleges, graduate schools, libraries, paperback books; we can afford the leisure—to visit art museums, to attend concerts and theatres, to travel. Whether we shall spend the money—to build more schools and libraries, concert halls and theatres, and to compensate our creative artists—remains largely a political question. Hopefully, it is a question to which at long last the politicians are giving some thought, if not as yet much action.

Finally, there is the most subtle of all these causes of the cultural explosion. Perhaps this one is unanalyzable. It is the changing image of the intellectual and of the artist in our society. Such men too were luxuries which frontier society could not support and which bourgeois provincial society could not understand and therefore would not tolerate. Even in our seemingly more enlightened 1940's and 1950's they remained suspect—eggheads, eccentrics, beatniks. Their image is beginning to change in the 1960's. To some extent the change is the result of a natural revulsion which Americans felt to the anti-intellectualism of the McCarthy investigations and to the intellectually barren national political administrations of that period. To a much larger extent it is the result of the stunning blow to the American ego administered by the Russians when they launched their sputnik in 1957. Of course the popular image of the American intellectual of the 1960's is an egghead in a space helmet, a scientist rather than a poet or an abstract painter. But science is an intellectual discipline, as are literature, music, and art. If they must remain separate, "two cultures," they nevertheless can flourish in peaceful coexistence.

The European in the 1960's contemplates American culture with a mixture of reactions. He is dazzled by its vigor and vitality in contrast to the tired, often jejune spirit of his own national culture. He is appalled by its pervasiveness, its bigness, and its overwhelming popular appeal. He may admire American jazz, but he is horrified to see his own young people turning to rock 'n' roll. He blames America for the cultural decline that he thinks he detects in his own country and talks gloomily about the sinister influences of American motion pictures and television, with their westerns, crime stories, inane situation comedies. Yet he will usually acknowledge, often with more enthusiasm than Americans themselves, that the American influence is endlessly stimulating. His novelists make no effort to conceal their indebtedness to Hemingway and Faulkner; his playwrights, their indebtedness to O'Neill, Arthur Miller, and Tennessee Williams. In the dance he will quickly admit that the choreography of Martha Graham, George Balanchine, and Jerome Robbins is revitalizing the whole ballet tradition; and if his knowledge of American composers is limited to musical comedies, he will nevertheless generously applaud the many touring American symphony conductors and concert artists. American painters like Jackson Pollock, Mark Tobey, and Willem de Kooning, while not widely known abroad, are viewed with attention and respect by European connoisseurs. The work of American architects like Frank Lloyd Wright and Edward Durell Stone has stimulated controversy, admiration, and emulation not only in Europe but in Asia and Latin America as well.

The American "image" is changing so rapidly that it can hardly be caught and held long enough at any fixed moment to be accurately described. One generalization, however, can be made with relative safety, and that is that American culture today is not exclusively American. It is international, both in its origins and in its effects. The views of two foreign observers of the current American cultural scene are represented in this first section. Both are informed, sympathetic, and candid. D. W. Brogan, British historian who has for many years been a student of American life, examines the roots of our "democratic culture" and shows a basic but not necessarily insoluble conflict between the leveling, popularizing tendencies of mass democratic society and the essentially aristocratic idea of excellence which is fundamental to any meaningful culture. Henri Peyre, a French scholar and critic, for many years a teacher in American universities, takes a close look at what will inevitably be the nucleus of America's cultural development—our institutions of higher learning. Here—in spite of the dangers of rapid expansion, bureaucratic administration, and overorganization—Professor Peyre finds an idealism, energy, and intellectual achievement unrivaled by any other country in the civilized world.

THE CHARACTER OF AMERICAN CULTURE[1]

"Culture" is a highly ambiguous term. However I may limit my definition of it, "culture" remains a wide term demanding for its full definition and illustration a range of knowledge that I do not possess.

Culture can have two meanings. There is the meaning given to the word by the anthropologist, in which all social habits, techniques, religious practices, marriage customs, in fact every-thing—including the kitchen sink—is examined to throw light on how a particular society lives and moves, or just exists. Then there is "culture" in a narrower sense, in which we are concerned not with material techniques, not with the social organization that holds society together, but with the ideas, the aesthetic ex-periences and achievements, and the philosophical or religious ideas that affect and are affected by the aesthetic experiences and achievements of a given society. A special variant of the last sense of "culture" is the narrow identification of the word with the fine arts and the implicit relegation of the fine arts to the margin of life, to what is done in leisure or for leisure.

None of these usages of the word is strictly separable from the others. The first usage obviously includes all the possible variations on the meaning and even the most restricted implies the wider meaning as a background. I shall not try, therefore, to attain a rigorous standard of definition or eschew all over-lapping of one definition of culture and another. I shall try to deal with the problem of the level and the tone of American culture in its second sense, but I shall not try to define that second sense narrowly or regard myself as debarred from using illustrations from American life that a culture snob would think showed a confusion of ideas or a lowering of standards. In my view culture that is merely a set of aesthetic practices, merely exemplified in private or even in public taste, is a theme of importance—to be treated by somebody else. What I am con-cerned with is the problem of cultural standards and achieve-ments in an advanced democratic society, specifically the United States. And that cultural achievement cannot be separated from religion, education, the character of the state, the general aims and ambitions of American society. . . .

[1] From *America in the Modern World*, by D. W. Brogan, British historian and political scientist. Rutgers University Press. New Brunswick, N.J. '60. Ch. V, p 87-107. Copyright © 1960 by Rutgers University Press. Reprinted by permission.

The cultural "mark" of American society . . . is the absence of a strong, received aristocratic tradition, on the one side, and, on the other, the presence of a number of what can loosely, in a social if not a purely political sense, be called "democratic" biases and practices. The fine arts, literature, music, the content of the higher education have from the beginning been affected by the general egalitarian, progressive, optimistic, factual, future-discounting tone of American life. As I shall have occasion to note later, this bias of American life has often produced a powerful reaction and some of the classics of American literature are in the nature of minority protests against just those marks of American society that I have stressed. Nevertheless, American culture, in its widest sense, has these marks and American culture in its narrower sense has them too, even if to many the marks appear as scars.

What in the beginning marked off the nascent American culture from that of Europe? One thing I would suggest was poverty, poverty in a society already more egalitarian than that of Europe. People came to America to get rich (among other reasons); they did not arrive rich. Establishing their culture beachheads on the eastern coast, they had not the resources of time or of energy for the reproduction on the American shore of the elaborate cultural life that some of them had shared and all of them had heard of in Europe. There was no demand for a Vandyke, an Inigo Jones, a Milton in seventeenth century America; no means of producing or sustaining such artists.

The contrast with Spanish America is striking in at least one field, that of architecture. The Spanish colonists had two resources that the English colonists lacked: a docile and utilizable Indian population and "treasure," gold and silver. There was from the first in Spanish America a surplus for the fine arts. There was more. There was a government and a church that both aimed at splendor and had the political resources to use the surplus to produce it. It was not only that in English America there were no easily exploitable human and material resources to permit the creation of a materially splendid society. There were no institutions to insist that such splendor should be provided. The royal government, the churches could not, even if they had wished, force the colonists to produce art works on the scale of the Cathedral of Mexico.

Dwelling houses, churches and public buildings were necessarily simple, utilitarian. They could be and sometimes were aesthetically satisfactory as well, but the aim was not splendor. It was utility. Simplicity often is a form of beauty and elegance, but I think that some harm is done to the modern American sense of the beautiful by too much insistence on the triumphs of a simplicity that was imposed by need rather than by choice. From the beginning beauty was associated in American experience with functional fitness. It is an admirable association and, if one has to choose, it is better to have functional fitness than irrelevant ornament, but a certain Puritanical indifference or hostility to mere beauty, mere ornament is or was part of the American inheritance.

"Puritanical." I am aware that the word is ambiguous and I have no intention of using it as a term of abuse. But it did matter that the predominant religious tradition of early English America was one that left little place for the *luxe pour Dieu* that produced the great cathedrals and abbeys of Europe. I am aware that English (and American) Puritans had a high and competent sense of the place of music in divine worship. Nevertheless, the new environment was not that provided by Rome for Palestrina or by Leipzig for Bach. Milton was a musically minded Puritan poet, but he would not have found much to gratify his tastes had he emigrated to New England or to Virginia.

And if the material and ideological obstacles to the transfer of the more lavish, extravagant and nonutilitarian forms of the arts to America did not work so effectually in the case of literature, the transfer had some special difficulties all the same. One was material; there was, again, no means of accumulating an economic surplus to support the career of letters. It was possible to export the old classical learning and equally important the old and new biblical learning and, what was more important, the Bible itself. And no people that had the Bible made available and treasured by the established order was cut off from the highest literary excellence. Yet again the colonies—with no theatres, no court, no court patronage, as yet no equivalent of the new academies like the Royal Society of London, with the new life constantly calling for new effort, with no leisure class—could not be expected to and did not produce a variegated, non-utilitarian, original culture in the arts or, indeed, in the sciences, in what was then called natural philosophy. It would be absurd to make this a matter of reproach. It was part of the price paid for the establishment of the peculiar and successful Anglo-American society out of which the United States and its present culture have come. All I should like to suggest is that there was a necessary price; it was paid.

I am now coming to a more controversial part of my subject, the character of this necessarily democratic culture. That the American culture, on its aesthetic and intellectual side, is democratic I shall try to show later. What I want to do at the moment is to stress its early nonaristocratic character. The European culture from which it stemmed had its democratic elements: its folk ballads dealing with the woes and happiness of the "lower orders," the "short and simple annals of the poor." It had in its material works of art plenty of scenes from vulgar life, on the porches of great cathedrals, or the illuminations of the *Hours* of the Duc de Berry. But the more splendid forms of artistic achievement in the Middle Ages, as in the Renaissance, were aristocratic. The great popular legends were of kings and queens, of princes and princesses, of knights, of crusades and battles, feuds in castles, not of their less interesting equivalents in cottages. No doubt there are signs of a protest against this concentration on the great. The Robin Hood legend is an example. But most people accepted the distinction. Poor French peasants passed on, with faith and admiration, the legend of the Four Sons of Aymon and even now it is legends of the higher feudalism that Sicilian peasants paint on their carts. They would have agreed with Calpurnia:

> When beggars die, there are no comets seen;
> The heavens themselves blaze forth the death of princes.

Now, the settlers brought out from Europe, more specifically from the British Isles, this aristocratic culture. (The Bible, after all, is full of kings and nobles; sinners most of them, but interesting sinners. The metaphorical language of the Bible is royal, not democratic.) But in the American environment the aristocratic culture, accepted and admired by the people, began to wither. The old ballads were brought over but were transformed, given an American, frontier-bred, forest-bred character.

The legends of kings and princes became legends of men of the people winning the endless war against the wilderness and the Indian. Robin Hood was a hero that could be transported to the frontier; Richard Coeur de Lion was not.

I attach great importance to the creation of this frontier folk epic, not only because it tells us of the formation of the modern American culture but because it is the greatest American cultural export. It should be remembered that it is English America that has produced the only universally accepted new epic theme. The "matter of America" is in the true succession from the "matter of France" (Roland and the Paladins) and the "matter of Britain" (King Arthur and the Knights of the Round Table).

It is a matter not of kings and great nobles but of the self-made men of the forest and later of the prairie; it is a democratic epic theme. As far as there is a genuine American national tradition of legend, this is it. I am not altogether convinced that scholars, as well as hard-pressed men of letters, have not invented some of the prestige of the frontier heroes. I know how the Buffalo Bill legend was created; I have suspicions about Paul Bunyan and Mike Fink; but even if the legend has undergone the shaping hand of the poet or the poetaster or the scholar, that is how great legends are given their final and effective traditional form. And the legend of the West is still living in America— and still exportable to Europe. The conquest of the TV screen by the West is conclusive proof of the power of the legend that for a time represented a fact and for longer met a need of the new American social culture, a need for heroes and heroic deeds in an American and egalitarian context. I should not assert that as an art form the way in which this legend has been given to the American public is one of the greatest human achievements. I doubt if even [James] Fenimore Cooper as a writer is in the class of his model, Scott. But the legend he launched on the world was unlike the legend Scott exported to Europe and America, a modern living legend with a future. It was a legend of heroes chosen not by birth but by themselves.

As far as American literary culture has been the embodiment of this heroic legend it has been one of the makers and the marks of the American national ethic. And I, for one, am not disposed to look this gift horse too closely in the mouth or to assess this national asset in a purely literary crucible. If (as I think is true) the American national hero who is most effectively cast in the epic mold and most excites the national curiosity, as well as admiration, is Lincoln, the lesson is reinforced, for here is the folk hero, coming from the folk, embodying in the highest power their possibilities of promotion and achievement. That is one way in which American culture is democratic.

There is another, one that is perhaps less edifying, less a pure acquisition. In a famous passage in his book on Hawthorne, Henry James stresses and laments the poverty of resources available to the American man of letters. Compared to his European brother, how little he has to use, how simple the social structure in which he is to set the characters! There is something comic in this long list of things that America has not got. It is, oddly enough, the converse of what Goethe had to say: he congratulated America on its escape from the feudal past that James coveted. And obviously James exemplified in his own work the possibilities of the new American theme contrasted with the old, traditional European themes. But there was something in the Jamesian lament, if not quite what James thought it was. For in the more sophisticated forms of literary art, the egalitarian bias of American life worked against the reception of the more subtle forms of art by the great American public—and there was no substitute for the great American public. There was no center of patronage, of support, of protection for the artist.

It is not necessary to swallow all the criticisms of American society fashionable with writers for over a hundred years— criticisms of the aridity of American culture, of the dry, inhospitable air in which the artist found it difficult to breathe— to recognize that, for some types of artist at any rate, nineteenth century America—busy building itself up, completing the conquest of the frontier, assimilating the vast immigrant floods— could not be, or at any rate was not, very hospitable to the arts.

It was perhaps not accidental that the "golden day" of New England marked not the first efflorescence of a culture but the sunset of the old, learned, theocratic New England way of life, the marriage of the old Puritan conscience with the optimism of the Enlightenment. Emerson, Hawthorne, and the lesser men, Holmes, Lowell and the rest, were fruits of a society declining and which owed its charm and some of its force to its nearly twilight character. There is something paradoxical in this situation and it is a paradox that many Americans refuse to face, but there it is. The New England culture, the best integrated, the most internally harmonious regional culture that America has known, knew its golden day only when its decline was imminent. "Minerva's owl flies only in the dusk," said Hegel, and this deep saying applies to Boston, Concord, Salem. And—a banality that I am almost ashamed to utter—the great figures of American literary culture have been on the whole hostile to or at any rate highly critical of American life. Emerson had his repeated bursts of optimism but the world in which he spent the second half of his life was a world that listened not at all to his deepest message. It is hardly necessary to stress the pessimism of Hawthorne or the ostentatious disillusionment of Henry Adams.

And it was not only the New Englanders who were disillusioned, cut off. Whitman alone kept his spirits up and it is to be doubted if his best poetry is really to be found in those paeans to the spirit of democracy, those laudations of "Pioneers, O Pioneers." For Mark Twain the human situation was incurably tragic and for Melville the human illusion inevitably led to a dead end:

> Round the world! There is much in that sound to inspire proud feelings, but whereto does all that circumnavigation conduct? Only through numberless perils to the very point whence we started, whence those we left behind secure, were all the time before us.

Could there be a more un-American attitude than Melville's (and there are other lessons to the same effect)?

Classical American literature is not notably "useful" in the narrow nationalist sense. It is useful in a deeper sense, as is any penetrating, truthful, moving insight into the human situation. But the average American—optimistic, energetic, convinced, despite Melville, that circumnavigation does conduct us somewhere and somewhere worth arriving at—was and is naturally put off by the insistence on the darker side of the American situation. He has too often despised and distrusted the artist who has reciprocated the attitude. Exiled even if he did not leave the territorial bounds of the United States, the artist, the philosopher, the pure scientist were both cut off and cut themselves off from the main, cheerful stream of national tradition.

Of course, the alienation of the artist was not purely an American problem. War on the bourgeoisie, on bourgeois ideals and practices, was one of the common slogans of European life, especially in France. But Dickens and Hugo, social critics as they were, were not cut off from the life of their age as were their American opposite numbers and they were and have remained effective national heroes as no American author, not even Mark Twain, has been.

The consequence has been a separation of what I am prepared to call the higher culture and the less original, more perishable, more optimistic, more American (in the patriotic sense) culture that has unfortunate results even today—or especially today.

Here it is necessary to say something of the picture of the American cultural past that American academics have been presenting not so much to the public as to the captive audiences of the colleges. Nothing could be more admirable from a moral as well as an intellectual point of view than the industry and the acuteness and probity with which American scholars have examined all the American past, the works of the great, the near great, and the merely "interesting." But here I take my life in my hands and, as a foreigner, I should like to suggest that in their desire to assess accurately the American cultural past they have tended to stress its utility for the American student to an excessive degree. The ordinary, intelligent, interested but not totally fascinated young man or woman who is introduced to the idea of literature as more than a mere diversion, as an illumination of life and not as a mere distraction from it, may find the great American classics depressing and the lesser lights, so laboriously resurrected or at any rate exhumed, both mediocre and boring. American literary culture is not varied enough (is especially not rich enough in first-class poetry) to provide adequate nutriment for the young.

In a legitimate attempt to prove the original value of the American contribution American critics and scholars, it seems to me, have tended to put blinkers round their charges, who might otherwise look out at the great world and discover there much that is profound, illuminating, and nourishing, even for Americans, but which has the handicap of having been written not by Americans nor for Americans but by human beings for human beings. It was the advantage of the old classical curriculum on which the New England masters were brought up that it enforced knowledge of nonnational, of remote types of human achievement, that it insinuated the idea of a common human experience that Homer and Vergil threw light on. Today only the Bible (as far as it is still read apart from being bought) performs that function.

Something of the same limitation arises in the study of other aspects of American culture. It was a misfortune that the great expansion of the United States, in area, in wealth, in ambition, came at a time when in all countries of the new machine world taste was at its lowest, most timid, least connected with the forces of real creation. It is not only in the United States that money was squandered in atrocious imitations of the "Gothic," in inappropriate revivals of the classical, in ingenious and learned but not very relevant exercises in the Romanesque. To repeat, the United States was not the only sufferer. Is there any worse piece of church building erected regardless of cost anywhere in the United States than the Sacré-Coeur in Montmartre? Germany, France, and England are full of railway stations, government buildings, town halls that cannot be exceeded for unbeautiful ingenuity in any American city. (And I have some peculiarly unlucky American cities in mind.) Yet in the European cities, as a rule, the past had left achievements that ought to have put the modern architects and patrons to shame.

In many American cities there was nothing to offset the extravagantly outrageous taste of the gilded age—or later. Of course, there were pioneers like Louis Sullivan and many American cities have buildings of the late nineteenth and the early twentieth century that architects from Europe go on pilgrimage to. But visually the United States boomed at a bad time. And we have here, I think, another cause of alienation between the American and the higher culture of his country and age.

What of it? Is his situation any worse than that of the representative Englishman or Frenchman? Do they admire and use the products of the highest culture in their age and country? Of course not. But the American is in a special position. He is in Henry James's America, where the background to the arts has to be created and assimilated, where democratic judgment is part of the national ethos, where reverence is a quality reserved for a few sacred political slogans and institutions, where the not totally harmful snob values of an aristocratic culture are absent. The American is left to himself, not only because he does not accept leaders but because many leaders will not lead. For that reason, and possibly for others, the American cultural scene is peculiarly divided, the national unity, so remarkable at other levels, is here almost totally missing.

On the one hand, the American willingness to try anything once aids the arts, aids the preacher of new aesthetic or social doctrine. Just as American law tolerates, to a degree that surprises the European visitor, unorthodox systems of medicine, just as every known form of religious belief gets a welcome, so every new form of the arts, every new theory, every new form of practice finds buyers, in both a financial and a psychological sense. If from one point of view America suffers by having no accepted standards of excellence, she gains in another by not being hidebound by accepted standards of excellence. The very absence of what I may call "normative" institutions is a blessing. At any rate, it may seem so when the role of the French Academy in one field and the English Royal Academy in another is contemplated.

Probably at no time in history has the seller of cultural goods had it so good, in the sense that buyers will not be choked off by a mere inability to understand what it is all about. In face of the claims of the new art forms, in literature, in music, in painting, in sculpture, even in architecture, millions of Americans act like so many Texans afraid not to buy a potential oil well. What is offered may be unintelligible and unattractive, but it may conceal a gusher all the same. (I hasten to say that I am not describing buyers who are looking for a cash capital gain, but buyers in the widest sense of the term, who do not want to miss what may be the great cultural revelation of the age.)

This hospitality applies not only to the arts but to other aspects of culture, and notably to religion and what may be called philosophy. The American who seeks deliverance in analysis or in some new psychological school, who wants to master Zen Buddhism in ten easy lessons is a direct descendant of the seekers after knowledge whom Emerson made fun of more than a century ago—but who provided Emerson with a great part of his audiences and readers. It is not the searching after new things that is new, it is the evaporation, in the century since the decline of the Transcendentalists, of the old orthodoxy against which Emerson and his brethren reacted.

Here, again, the American situation is not unique. All over the Western world the seekers are as numerous as in St. Paul's Athens and the doctrines offered are much more varied. I am reduced to uttering a platitude when I stress the speed and diversity of change in our contemporary world. Our picture of it is changing so fast that it is vain to look for a central core of doctrine round which we can arrange our cultural life. If the modern world has such a core, a central and triumphant discipline, it is in physics, and who that is not quite a respectable mathematician can even begin to grasp what the physicists are doing? We can grasp in general what their allies and pupils, the engineers, are doing. Each new satellite, each new threat of more murderous rocketry, keeps them in our mind and we know that they can provide the means for destroying us. We are all in the Western world in the same cultural boat, in a world we never made where old patterns are dissolving and changing too fast for us to adjust easily or comfortably or even to decide what we should adjust to.

But what is different in the American situation is first of all the democratic tradition of culture which I have briefly described. The old traditional order of a "higher" culture handed down from above—representing overtly aristocratic values or, at any rate, being based on the premise that some forms of culture are superior to others and that superiority is not simply an aspect of their popularity—is probably dying in Europe. But it is not yet dead. It visibly survives in the curriculum of the schools, in the prestige still attached to traditional hierarchical values, and (this is a matter where nothing but intuition can be relied on) in a genuine humility before the claims of the traditional culture that produces a willingness to learn that in turn results, in a good many cases, in a genuine conversion to the standards of a higher culture and a genuine appreciation of its products.

It is true that this acceptance of the traditional culture, this docile readiness to be initiated into it as far as natural talents and acquired knowledge make it possible, is not quite that immersion in the highest things that the preachers of culture, Matthew Arnold and T. S. Eliot, have meant. Nevertheless, the attitude preserves the older culture long enough for it to be possible to hope that a new culture, fusing the best of old and new, may arrive before general barbarism does.

The 800,000 copies of a translation of the *Odyssey* sold in England may not represent a genuine readiness to put oneself in the way of understanding of a remote way of life or a willingness to see and feel the human situation in another form from that to which we are habituated. But they do represent something that, faced with the products of the lower culture, with rock 'n' roll and the comics, we may be inclined to forget does exist.

If (as I think is the case) much of the pessimism of the "intellectuals" in America, in Britain, in Europe, arises from the collapse of the hopes based on the democratization of society, the end of the belief that the only things needed to win the masses to the higher culture were leisure, abundance, more "education," cheap books as well as the novel possibilities of radio and TV, then it is worth while to remind ourselves that not all those hopes were vain.

It is even more dangerous to blind ourselves to the facts of our situation (here I include both Britain and the United States in a common dilemma). We can do this in a new way as well as in the old way that asserted that we all must needs love the better when we see it. We can persuade ourselves that the new popular art forms are the natural successors of the old art forms, that they represent an inevitable adjustment to a new form of society. Thus rock 'n' roll is a necessary reflection of contemporary malaise; Li'l Abner, the equivalent of the great popular authors of the past, of Mark Twain and Dickens. If the boys and girls who pour out from high schools don't want to read, in a sense can't read, the reflection is on the absurd prestige we attach to reading or on the absurd and irrelevant reading matter issued to the aspiring young and their turning to other art forms than literature.

There is some plausibility in all these defenses of abdication in favor of popular adolescent taste. I think it likely that the literary arts may be giving way in prestige, perhaps in cultural utility, to other arts, to the plastic arts and, above all, to music. Music, I think, has become the refuge of the intelligent man and woman today and that not because hi-fi has enabled him to gratify his tastes but because those tastes have produced the market for hi-fi. I think that a timid reverence for "classics" may mean that school reading programs have a diseducative effect, since serious reading becomes associated with boredom. And in any group of intelligent boys and girls there are sure to be young men and young women of whom some have no more an eye for reading than others have an ear for music, or others the ability to do simple sums.

But the present cultural crisis is not concerned with these cases. It is right to discriminate among comics, to point out the superiority of "Li'l Abner" over records of violence, empty of ideas, for example. It is right to insist on the technical superiority of a great jazz performer like Louis Armstrong over the current wailers and moaners. These last may enable a great many of the young to express themselves vicariously, but it is a dangerous extension of democratic prejudice to assert that all forms of self-expression are commendable or equally admirable and promising. It is wrong and a "treason of the learned" to exalt the art forms that are most popular today simply because they are popular in merely numerical terms. "Dare to be a Daniel" was the message of a popular hymn. "Dare to be a square" is a motto I should like to see adopted by more academics and other ex officio molders of the public mind.

The reasons why this motto is not adopted are various. One is the division, at any rate in the literary field, between the temper of the greatest American artists and the national temper. The national temper is optimistic, still deeply impressed by the belief in progress and still prone to believe that somewhere a solution can be found, if we try hard enough, for the temporarily distressing human condition. Yet this was not and is not the temper of the most critically esteemed American writers and to be a devoted admirer of Mr. Faulkner, for example, is to be in that degree un-American.

Then there is a division between the more sophisticated artists and the aspiring public that I believe to be greater than in any historical period known to me. Again, this division is not confined to the United States; it is a chasm in all the Western countries. Literature, the visual arts, music, philosophy are all practiced at a high degree of sophistication by highly trained specialists. They are also studied and appreciated by highly sophisticated devotees. But much of the production of the modern artist (using the term in its widest connotation) makes small or no appeal to the average man, not even to the intelligent average man who is conscious that his life would be fuller and better if the arts spoke more loudly to him than they do.

I have said that this division is new. I do not believe that in the thirteenth and fourteenth centuries all the good Catholic worshippers appreciated the scholastic philosophers or fully understood the achievement of Chartres. The *Divine Comedy* and the *Summa* were not popular works or within the reach of everybody. Nor do I believe that all Athenians knew by what divine skill the Parthenon gots its proportions or appreciated all that Sophocles meant or were fit to be admitted to the Academy. I could multiply the examples.

But I think the modern situation is different. What a very modern musician means by music or a very modern nonrepresentational artist means by painting or many modern writers mean by literature has only a remote and often invisible connection with what the average sensual man means by these arts. I am aware that public taste has to be educated, that there were people who thought Mozart hard to follow and definitely discordant, that there were people who thought the Impressionists were simply incompetent. Maybe it is going to be like that for all the arts now in such confusion, now cut off, as so often they are, from what used to be their normal audience.

Even if we are all going to make the grade we haven't made it yet, and the average man is tempted, not unreasonably, to throw his hand in. He may exalt the claims of various jazz schools to be art forms as rich as classical music and its heirs or he may deny that classical music has any legitimate heirs. He may see or profess to see in fine camera work the true succession to the great painters, in the engineers the fit heirs of the architects. He may abandon pure literature altogether as a means of spiritual refreshment and turn to history, geography, travel, "know-how" books for more information. If he does so he will be in grave danger of reinforcing in himself the innate American belief that George Santayana commented on, the confidence in quantity, the preference for things that can be measured, the emphasis on more rather than on better, the identification of more *with* better. In our world emphasis on number, on measurable magnitudes, is one of the necessities of life, a necessity that presses ever more hardly on us.

But a life based on a belief that all that should be valued can be measured is like a life based on the belief that all that has to be learned can be taught. It is doomed to emotional sterility and to a sense of deception. Life is not like that and it is painful to find this out too late. What is missing in that life is what I have already alluded to in my remarks on education—the sense of excellence.

The danger to the notion of excellence does not lie only in the irrelevant emphasis on measurable quantity. It can and often does lie in the attribution to mediocrity of the power and prestige of excellence. Here, again at the risk of uttering platitudes, I have to join in the attack on the mass media. For it is possible to argue that they do less harm in their exaltation of the palpably trivial and transitory than in the excessive seriousness with which minor triumphs in the lively arts are greeted. That these lively arts can be diverting I do not deny. So can detective stories, so can much light and some low literature. I do not shudder at a *Saturday Evening Post* cover or wince when I hear of the prices paid for tickets to a fashionable musical.

But a lot of harm is done when a great popular success like *South Pacific* or *My Fair Lady* is puffed up until the distinction between talent and genius is lost sight of, between the work to which one may give the adjective "immortal" with no pedantic scruple and commercial productions of high amusement value that are extremely unlikely to survive the generation that welcomed them. It is not a question of commercial motive. Shakespeare and Molière were both highly commercial men of the theatre. It is a question of not giving the rank of a masterpiece to what is simply agreeable, for if you do that you cannot savor the real masterpieces—which is a great loss to the individual and in the aggregate to the national culture. *My Fair Lady* is not *The Marriage of Figaro; By Love Possessed* is not *War and Peace* or *The Ambassadors*.

What I am pleading for is the presentation to the young of the concept that there is such a thing as excellence, that the unexamined life, the emotionally banal life, the life animated by a religion of mere good works and with no philosophy behind it, is inferior to the fuller life of the artist, the philosopher, the saint. And since most of us cannot be any of these things, the next best thing for us is the humble, industrious, and informed admiration for these great achievements of the human spirit.

This is, above all, the function of the universities. To them come a high proportion of the young people who are capable of this initiation. It is against these young people that so much in the modern world—not only in the American modern world but especially in the American modern world—conspires. They need fortification; they need knowledge imparted without pedantry but also without any easy submission to the taste of the hour or the natural laziness of the human mind. The United States has probably never known a period in which its cultural prestige was greater, in literature, in painting, in music, but the achievements that win the respectful interest of the outside world are not those that the mass of the American people (including congressmen in that mass) understand or are likely to understand.

A society that in addition to its immense economic and technical prestige has the prestige of being hospitable to the new, the original, the fruitful in the arts, that welcomes new ideas as well as new gimmicks, has an immense advantage in the contest for men's minds. It is not the novelty of the offerings so much as the possibility of novelty that wins the doubtful faced as an alternative with dogmatism, irrelevant domination of the arts by politics, the regular search for a safe common denominator. There is no such common denominator that is compatible with excellence. The notion of excellence is in this sense undemocratic, but it is not un-American. It was certainly an idea dear to Jefferson and to Lincoln. It will suffice if American public opinion and its official organs remember that "every man hath business and desire such as it is."

American life will be richer and more seductive if it permits and encourages the really exceptional, the really original man to pursue his bent, of course allowing for the fact that there will be phonies and flops at least as often as men of genius or even of remarkable talent. But this waste is one of the luxuries that the United States can now afford. And it must afford it if its way of life is to compete at all levels with that of its rival. It can compete on the technical level (if the United States goes all out). It can compete hands down at the level of popular diversion for, as we know, the iron curtain can hardly keep out

American popular music and I suspect that the comics would please millions behind the curtain. But it is not merely as an instrument in the cold war that I urge a bold and possibly offensive insistence on excellence. It is because the great success story of the American people deserves excellence in every human activity. It would be unworthy of the people who have wrought the American miracle in so many fields to settle for less.

A great triumph of the American spirit would be the fostering of a literary and artistic culture that freely took in all the contributions of its ancestral cultures, confident that to be American is to be not exclusive but welcoming and that Shakespeare and the Bible play a greater part in the making of American culture than Melville, than even Mark Twain. It will be most American when it is most universal.

HIGHER EDUCATION IN THE UNITED STATES [2]

Americans may pass for a boastful people, prone to deliver sermons and admonitions to the rest of the world and replete with self-assurance as to their achievement and their wisdom in eschewing the entanglements of the Old World or the adolescent revolutionary impulses of Asia and South America. But such complacent arrogance, if it ever existed, has been dealt hard blows in the last few decades. In no realm perhaps are Americans so assailed with doubts as in that of education. Parents nod their heads envying the schools of Britain, France, Germany, nay, of Russia; school principals hold schools of Europe up to us as paragons of greater intellectual achievement; college presidents look up nostalgically at the venerable halls of Oxford and Cambridge, at Heidelberg and at the Sorbonne, at institutions where alumni do not have to be cajoled into becoming donors and where the customer is not necessarily right, especially when the customer is a sophomore. Faculties in America are houses divided against themselves, even more than elsewhere; they change their minds and their votes easily, they experiment, they try reforms which they forget having already tried ten years earlier and found wanting. Students are often afflicted with a vague inferior-

[2] From "Higher Education in the United States," from *Observations on Life, Literature, and Learning in America* by Henri Peyre. Copyright © 1961 by Southern Illinois University Press. Reprinted by permission of Southern Illinois University Press Carbondale. p 219-33. Henri Peyre is a professor of French at Yale University.

ity complex where European education is concerned. From Woodrow Wilson when he assumed the presidency of Princeton University to Robert Maynard Hutchins at Chicago, from journalists like Walter Lippmann to historians like Arthur Bestor and George Kennan, the critics of American education have been and are legion. They are more vocal, and they are more soberly heeded by the public at large, than in any other country. . . .

If we . . . turn to a consideration of American higher education, by which we mean undergraduate teaching at its best and graduate teaching and research, we find that self-criticism, which is and should be the life blood of anything pertaining to education and to science, is equally unsparing; but fairness demands that we place such criticism, at times ironical and condescending, at other times devastating and even masochistic, in its true perspective. Higher education today in America, as a whole, is second to none; research in the sciences, in the social disciplines, but also in literary history and criticism, in philosophy, in art history stands today, for its quantitative output and for its average quality, at the top of any country.

Some of the reasons for a truly striking achievement need only be recalled briefly: unequaled material resources, part of which (never adequate, yet substantial) has been devoted to research and advanced education; the healthy rivalry of centers of learning scattered over the country, vying with each other to attract money and brains, to create a spirit favorable to research; the mobility characteristic of the American people, their distrust of routine, of conservatism, of academics, their reluctance to turn universities into self-reproductive institutions. To those and other factors must be added the shrewd and generous impulse which has invited those scholars and scientists who were threatened in Europe to make their homes in America. . . .

American research in all branches of knowledge has, in the last three decades, won the respect of the world. Its preeminence is in part due to the ample means placed at its disposal: close to 20 per cent of a total sum of two billion spent on higher education, public and private, is allotted to organized research, as against 5 per cent (of a smaller total) twenty years ago. Such funds are provided, directly or indirectly, by Federal agencies, by foundations or by industry. That research is conspicuously free from control. The spirit of free inquiry is in no way curbed.

Yet, insidiously but not perfidiously, research in the sciences and in the social sciences can be inspired by the sources which provide the funds. Attention is directed toward some problems while others are temporarily neglected. Teamwork is often overemphasized. The "curse of bigness" hangs over donating institutions: it is easier for foundations to allot one million dollars to one team than a hundred times ten thousand dollars to as many individuals or projects. Hence the temptations to inflate some projects and to apply for sizable, or colossal, grants.

Big projects imply the mushrooming of committees, subcommittees, executive assistants, deputy executive assistants, deputy vice presidents and all the paraphernalia of organizational society as mockingly denoted by Parkinson's law. A good deal of the time which professors should devote to their research is taken up by serving on committees, as if, beyond a certain age, their colleagues feared that scientists might have few novel ideas and scholars had better not write. Executives in a quandary act like the statesman whose difficulties are pathetically described in the second part of T. S. Eliot's *Coriolan:*

> Cry cry what shall I cry?
> The first thing to do is to form the committees:
> The consultative councils, the standing committees,
>   select committees and sub-committees.

A solution might appear to lie in the development of a separate class of organizers of research and of administrators of universities, on the assumption that those combats with the unknown, or with demons, are too important to be left to professors. Therein however lies another peril: politics is to be run very differently from business and education is a human, all too human affair. Lecturers are sometimes prima donnas; researchers are temperamental dreamers who chafe at an excess of efficiency around them, cannot work at regular hours and profit most from dreaming or observing with the nonchalant freedom of imagination. An excess of organization of advanced research can be detrimental to the boldness and freedom of inquiring minds. "Ever let the Fancy roam!" Keats' line can be meaningful also for scientists and for scholars.

Many scientific visitors from South America and Europe have commented upon their American experiences and their reflections have usually concurred on this: that the most impressive assets of research in this country are not the material means or the efficiency in organizing, but the confident trust of people in one another and the spirit of cooperation. There prevails a greater faith in one's fellow beings in this vast continent, including one's fellow scientists. Envy, cantankerousness, jealousy of the young, secrecy practiced to one's research assistants and secretaries are less often to be encountered than they are in older lands.

Some nationalism has lately sprung up among musical composers and artists, who have attempted to play down the arts of Europe in order to proclaim the vitality of their own creations; it has not carried much conviction with it. In general, American science and scholarship have become sufficiently self-assured to afford to be generously open to what comes from abroad. Americans realize how much they owe to the variety of their ethnic origins and open their facilities, provide their research and fellowship funds to persons of other nationalities. They have done so in exemplary fashion in the Fulbright program of Exchange of Persons. They have benefited Europe in doing so, and, for the first time in world history, they have treated their own wealth, in Carnegie's words, as a sacred trust to be used in the interest of other peoples. They have also benefited themselves. The truest friendships among nations are those which have been formed by the gifted individuals of those nations when, in their receptive youth, eager to observe what was foreign to them, fraternally open to what was different, they made a prolonged stay in another country, saw people at work, learned to appreciate their achievement and returned home broadened by their experience. To be the man only of one country, of one culture and of one age is to be less than a complete man.

II. AMERICAN CULTURE: AS WE SEE OURSELVES

EDITOR'S INTRODUCTION

A decade before people began talking about the cultural "boom" and the cultural "explosion" they were using these same words to describe the enormous increase in the birthrate during and just after World War II. Population explosions and birthrate booms are not as unrelated to culture as they might appear to be. The postwar period in America ushered in an all-pervasive sense of "bigness"—big families, big cars and airplanes, wider screens in motion picture theatres and on home television sets. The neighborhood grocery store became a supermarket; the local laundry became a launderama.

More children mean more potential customers and more potential artists and patrons of the arts. At the outset, they mean more schools and colleges. A glance at the statistics gathered by the United States Office of Education and the National Education Association offers dramatic evidence. In the period 1960-1962 nearly 30 per cent of the American population was involved in the educational process—51 million of them students; 2 million, teachers and administrators; two hundred thousand, trustees of various school systems. These figures do not include the millions of adults who are informally involved in educating themselves in extension and correspondence courses, discussion and seminar groups like the Great Books programs, television courses, or independent reading of the vast numbers of self-help, do-it-yourself books that are flooding the market, especially in paperback form. Nor do they suggest the great expansion of public library usage— not only in large urban and rapidly growing suburban areas, but also in small communities and isolated rural areas where, since the passage by Congress in 1956 of the Library Services Act, Federal grants-in-aid have helped to strengthen facilities. In 1961 the American Library Association Reading Survey reported that adult book circulation in libraries had increased 20 per cent in the past five years, with the reading emphasis shifting from westerns and mysteries to books on art, music, political affairs, science and technology.

Furthermore, an upward trend in the circulation of "literate" magazines has been detected. While the "little magazine" that published quality poetry and fiction has all but vanished under the pressures of inflation, the mass circulation weeklies like *Life* and *Look* have given increasing amounts of space to art reproductions and "guest" articles by eminent scholars, critics, and creative writers. Names like Arnold Toynbee, Bertrand Russell, Albert Camus, and Jean-Paul Sartre have appeared from time to time among the contributors to popular American magazines. Subjects like existentialism and the Dead Sea Scrolls have had more than passing attention in the mass media. Ernest Hemingway's novella *The Old Man and the Sea* reached an audience of staggering size on its first publication, which was in *Life* magazine. Sunday supplements in the newspapers are devoting considerable space to coverage of local, national and international cultural matters— books, art, records, theatre.

Before we can congratulate ourselves, however, on the new "Golden Age," the flowering of American culture, we must pause to consider the question of quantity versus quality. How many of the thousands who patiently queued up for hours to get a glimpse of the "Mona Lisa" when it was exhibited in Washington, D.C. and in New York early in 1963 were genuine art lovers? How many were drawn in simply by curiosity and the ballyhoo of publicity which the visiting painting received? How many who, eighteen months earlier, had formed similar queues to see Rembrandt's "Aristotle Contemplating the Bust of Homer" were lured not by the painting but by the record-breaking sum of $2.3 million which the Metropolitan Museum had paid for it? How many of the thousands of students clamoring for college admission are ardent for education, and how many merely seek the social and economic status which a college degree theoretically offers? How good is American public education? How good are our colleges, our universities, our graduate schools? True, more Americans are reading more books than ever before. But is culture necessarily the aim of their reading? Surveying the best sellers of 1960, Alice P. Hackett of *Publishers' Weekly* observed a great disparity between the sale of fiction, i.e., creative, imaginative literature, and nonfiction, and concluded that "the bookstore customer is inclined to buy books for information rather than for entertainment."

Of the quantity of American culture there is clearly no dispute. The statistics assembled by Alvin Toffler in his *Fortune* article reprinted in this section, by the *Business Week* survey of the sale of paperback books, by the New York *Times* report on attendance at museums offer weighty, indeed staggering evidence. But does the quality of American culture in the sixties match the quantity? Many observers of the current scene regard the cultural explosion with alarm and dismay. Karl E. Meyer, in his report for the *New Statesman*, cites the assembly-line aspects of "manufactured" popular culture, and quotes in support of his position Dwight Macdonald, who coined the phrases "Masscult" and "Midcult" to describe the ominous leveling effects of the cultural explosion. Ernest van den Haag in his "Reflections on Mass Culture" similarly warns against the mediocrity which characterizes large-scale popular culture and which tends to submerge the culturally elite minority.

Statistics are meaningful but sometimes misleading. Equally significant perhaps are the observations of thoughtful individuals who hesitate to indulge in premature self-congratulation on America's cultural upsurge, but who nevertheless detect a wholesome democratic trend in these facts and figures. The sociologist Edward Shils, in his study "Mass Society and its Culture" (*Daedalus*, Spring 1960), observes that the culture of a mass society is a reflection of the whole nature of our present-day industrial civilization. The broadening and leveling effects of such a society tend to produce an expansion of the mediocre and conventional trends in a culture, rather than "the notion of excellence" of which D. W. Brogan speaks in his essay on American culture (reprinted in Section I, above). Nevertheless, Professor Shils finds that "the evidence of decline is not by any means very impressive," and that, on the contrary, in every field of intellectual activity modern society is as productive as its predecessors. If the culturally elite, those who are dedicated to "the notion of excellence," remain aloof, in chilly isolation, issuing gloomy prophecies on the mass "brutalization" of culture, such a decline will come. But if, as Professor Roy Harvey Pearce suggests, in his article reprinted in this section, they will energetically engage themselves in the cause of a genuine popular culture, they will preserve and indeed enhance the values for which they are battling.

The popularization of art is a case in point. John Canaday, writing of the boom in private art collecting, reminds us that the Sears, Roebuck customers who are venturing into this field are hardly more naïve and dependent upon the connoisseurship of a taste-maker than were the wealthy art collectors of half a century ago who relied unquestioningly on their Berensons and Duveens. Even the most modest purchase of a reproduction of a great painting or a casual and occasional visit to a museum is better than indifference to art. Habits may be formed, especially among the young. Of the thousands who flock to their public libraries to seek practical information, some few may browse and pick up a novel or even a volume of poetry. Of the many schools and colleges expanding and springing up all over the country, not all are merely glorified vocational training centers. And many a student who goes to high school or college today simply because his parents can afford to send him stays to get a real education.

It is perhaps in its less spectacular and sensational forms that American culture in the sixties is finding its best and soundest expression. If so, it will not be until the seventies or even later that it can be accurately evaluated. Viewed practically and realistically, "mass" culture, whatever its potential risks, is a phenomenon unique to American society. If the phrase means anything at all, as Alfred Kazin has remarked, "it means the ever-widening social opportunity without which so many American intellectuals would have remained in the 'masses.'"

A QUANTITY OF CULTURE [1]

To the unprepared visitor it was a strange scene. In one corner Mrs. Glyde Scribner, a Minnetonka, Minnesota, pharmacist, hurled a lump of red clay fiercely to the floor, picked it up tenderly, examined it, then slammed it to the ground once more. Again and again she repeated this procedure until, winded, she set the shapeless mass on a high table in front of her, beamed at it, and caught her breath. This performance—known to sculptors as "wedging" clay—occasioned no surprise among the dozen other

[1] From article by Alvin Toffler, free-lance writer. *Fortune.* 64:124-7+. N. '61. Reprinted from the November 1961 issue of *Fortune* Magazine by Special Permission; © 1961 Time Inc.

people in the room, for they, like Mrs. Scribner, had all come to the Minnetonka Center of Arts and Education for an evening of ceramic sculpture. There, while a radio tuned to WLOL-FM filled the room with the strains of Bach's *Cantata No. 140,* they molded and modeled statues, plaques, and birdbaths under the watchful eye of an instructor borrowed from the College of St. Catherine in nearby St. Paul.

To the Minnetonka Center, founded in 1951 and currently housed in a small stucco-and-frame building set by the side of a tree-lined road, come over six hundred suburbanites to paint, sculpt, study creative writing, and, in general, pursue the arts. They include doctors, dentists, retired executives, a smattering of elderly spinsters, and, of course, the energetic Mrs. Scribner.

About a mile down the road from the center is a somewhat less elevated establishment—a beer joint. Its façade wears two large metal signs proclaiming it to be "Minnetonka's Fun Spot." Inside, a customer can not only drink Hamm's beer and listen to an earsplitting jukebox, he can buy original oil paintings from those on display on the walls for prices as high as $350.

These two institutions, each in its own modest way, symbolize a major transformation in the tastes and interests of Americans. A generation ago H. L. Mencken could characterize vast stretches of the United States as a "Sahara of the Bozart" and Carol Kennicott, repining, found that to be "artistic" or "high-brow" along Main Street was considered "priggish and of dubious virtue." Now the United States is experiencing a cultural surge of truly unprecedented proportions, which began shortly after World War II, gathered momentum during the early 1950's, and, in the last few years, has washed into the least likely corners of the land. Naturally, observers of American culture are eager to understand the meaning of this movement. Among cultural critics and social historians a vehement discussion is raging as to whether the new interest in the arts is good, bad, or merely superficial. . . .

We don't intend to get into the argument but, while it rages, merely to record some of the statistics and factual material about this cultural upsurge in the United States—how "big" it is, how it is organized, what it costs. It is even coloring management decisions. Whatever its meaning, this phenomenon has had a remarkable effect upon this fruitful and unpredictable continent.

The Price Tag

To start at the least qualitative point (the dollar sign), the sheer expenditure on cultural activities is impressive. Nobody can say with precision where the lines of culture begin and where they end. But within an area of rough agreement the figures are startling. For example, Americans in 1960 spent nearly $300 million just to operate their 620 art museums. How much more they poured into their 3,300 historical, scientific, and other nonart museums is an unknown but clearly sizable sum. Americans also laid out over $300 million to run their public libraries. They spent some $200 million to buy paintings, prints, color reproductions, and art materials for professional and amateur fine-arts use. They bought $90 million worth of recordings of classical music; they also spent $590 million for musical instruments and $26 million to operate their symphony orchestras—not counting those connected with schools and colleges. Their bill for books ran to at least $1 billion, a figure large enough to leave an impressive sum even after subtracting all the textbooks, westerns, and whodunits. They spent about $375 million at theatre, opera, and concert-hall box offices.

Exactly how much more they spent for art and music education in the schools, or for watercolor instruction and ballet lessons outside the schools, is impossible to know. And no one knows how many millions are being spent to run the literally hundreds of art centers, like the one in Minnetonka, that have sprouted up in wild profusion across the nation in the past decade. Americans spent or donated, all together, a rock-bottom minimum of $3 billion for culture last year, a figure that excludes public funds and business gifts. The significant point is that this sum is 70 per cent more than the comparable estimate for ten years ago.

All this has meant profitable times for those companies that directly feed the appetite for the arts (musical instrument makers, for example). But many companies that never thought of themselves as having any business with culture are surprised to discover that they have become patrons of the arts. Others find the yearning for culture affecting decisions in the fields of personnel recruiting and plant location. Many job applicants not only want to know what fringe benefits go with the job, they want to know what cultural advantages there will be for them and their children in the community. In trying to attract personnel, says J. C. Whitaker, a director of the R. J. Reynolds Tobacco Co. in Winston-Salem, "we make it a point to mention the many cultural groups in our city." In Cincinnati, Procter & Gamble mails a booklet describing local cultural events to young men it is seeking to recruit. IBM's choice of Rochester, Minnesota, San Jose, California, and Westchester, New York, as locations for new installations was influenced by the existence of lively cultural institutions in these places. Pat Touchae, a former mayor of Waterloo, Iowa, remembers that a couple of years ago his town "tried like the dickens to attract a certain industry here and it ended up in another Iowa city where there was a well-developed cultural program, including an art gallery and theatre." Since then, Waterloo has worked hard to develop local cultural activities.

The Concrete Expression

The most conspicuous expressions of America's new culture consciousness are the structures now abuilding in many cities to house cultural institutions. New York, of course, is building its $142 million Lincoln Center for the Performing Arts to house the Metropolitan Opera, the New York Philharmonic, the Juilliard School of Music, and other institutions. St. Paul is close to realizing its goal of $2.5 million for a handsome new downtown arts-and-science building. These are only two examples among impressive projects that include a new $24 million Music Center in Los Angeles, a cultural center based around Wayne State University in Detroit, a $500,000 arts center in Lynchburg, Virginia.

Museums, starting up at an average rate of one every four days for the last twenty-nine years, now number 3,900. In 1932 there were twelve museums in the United States for each million of population. Today there are twenty-two. The increase in the number of museums reflects "demand" as measured by attendance. A survey of twenty-one museums showed their combined 1958 attendance to be 19,370,000. By 1960 this had climbed more than 10 per cent to 21,360,000. The Metropolitan Museum of Art in New York chalked up a 17 per cent increase between 1958 and 1960. The Solomon R. Guggenheim Museum, devoted largely to abstract art, opened its doors in 1959 and was jammed by 939,000 visitors in its first year; some days the queues stretched for blocks. When the Detroit Institute of Arts unveiled its magnificent exhibition of Flemish masterpieces last winter, it clocked 105,000 viewers, 60,000 of whom paid admission for the privilege of viewing the Van Eycks and Van der Weydens.

Libraries, too, are doing a thriving business. The number of volumes in public libraries has increased from 143 million in 1950 to 210 million in 1960. Nor were these volumes just gathering dust. Total public library circulation reached 677 million volumes in 1958, and has been going up ever since. And readers were buying as well as borrowing, as the $1 billion spent for books attests. At the rate that book buying has been increasing, according to a study prepared for the Book Manufacturers' Institute, Americans will be purchasing—and presumably reading—1.2 billion books a year by 1965.

Crescendo

Americans were listening, as well, in a cultivated way. According to Helen Thompson, executive secretary of the American Symphony Orchestra League, the increase in symphony attendance in recent years has been nothing short of "phenomenal." Attendance at the Detroit Symphony Orchestra, for example, rose from 300,000 to 700,000 a year in the last decade. With this kind of encouragement, new orchestras have formed at a rapid rate and old ones have increased the length of their seasons. In 1950 there were approximately 800 orchestras in the United States; today there are 1,200, and most of the new ones have cropped up in cities with 50,000 population or less. In all, these orchestras played about 7,800 performances last year before an estimated total attendance of 10 million.

The Metropolitan Opera Association (whose 1961-1962 season was saved by the intervention of the Secretary of Labor) last year played to over 96 per cent of capacity during a lengthened season in New York, and played to virtually 100 per cent of capacity during its nine-city tour of places like Birmingham, Alabama, and Bloomington, Indiana. There are now in the United States 750 opera-producing groups, either professional or amateur. The Detroit Opera Theatre, started only two years ago, was successful in staging opera in English, including such infrequently performed works as Douglas Moore's *Gallantry,* and Donizetti's *The Night Bell.* The Dallas Civic Opera Company, founded in 1957, will put on six performances this season in a 4,200-seat hall.

At the same time, Americans were thronging record stores, buying last year 25 million long-playing disks of what not long ago was derisively termed "longhair stuff." This represented a 78 per cent increase over the comparable figure only three years ago. Moreover, the fifties saw a spectacular rise in amateur music making. The number of instrumentalists soared, and the dollar volume of instrument sales was up 150 per cent.

A newer wave of mass interest has shaken the world of painting and sculpture. Ten years ago there were about 150 art galleries in New York and perhaps an equal number spread thinly across the country, nearly all in the larger cities. Today there are over 300 galleries in New York alone, and nobody has counted the hundreds that have popped up in places like Flint, Michigan, and Quincy, Illinois. In Phoenix, Arizona, according to Dr. F. M. Hinkhouse, director of the Phoenix Art Museum, there were two galleries in 1950, four in 1955. The four did a combined business estimated at $100,000. Today, says Dr. Hinkhouse, there are at least fifteen galleries with an estimated volume of $1,500,000.

Galleries range from old and richly impressive Fifty-seventh Street emporiums like Knoedler's to a new kind of suburban or semisuburban gallery like Detroit's Raven Gallery, which opened its doors in July, 1960. The Raven is a store-front operation nestling in a quiet residential neighborhood. Started on a shoestring of $5,000 by a former printer named Herbert Cohen, the gallery sells sculpture and paintings for from $10 to as much as $2,300, all the work of Michigan artists. To attract the public, Cohen stages chamber-music recitals and discussions on cultural subjects for broadcast on WQRS, a local FM station. He serves patrons pastries and coffee. In its first year the Raven had 40,000 visitors.

The National Art Materials Trade Association estimates that the number of Sunday painters rose from 30 million in 1950 to 40 million in 1960—although this would seem to be one of the Unknowable Statistics. . . . The breadth and variety of the amateur movement are illustrated by what happened in 1957 when a young woman producer suggested that KQED, a San Francisco educational TV station, air a half-hour program about Japanese brush painting. Since it was to be a "how-to" program, she thought of selling brush-painting kits to interested viewers. Accordingly, she bought 300 sets and exhibited them at the end of the program. "Frankly," says James Day, general manager of the station, "I was skeptical. I told her I hoped she had made arrangements to return all the sets she couldn't sell." The program has since been sold to fifty-three other TV channels around the country, and 14,000 sets have been sold at $3 each.

Theatres Everywhere

The Broadway theatre may be somewhat anemic, but elsewhere a very vigorous theatre has sprung up. New York's off-Broadway playhouses have grown from a handful in 1950 to thirty-two last year, when, according to Paul Libin of the League of Off-Broadway Theaters and Producers, they took in an estimated $3 million from nearly one million patrons. Outside New York, professional resident acting companies have been formed in cities like Pittsburgh, Milwaukee, Houston, Washington, San Francisco. According to *Variety,* there are also now about 5,000 nonprofessional theatre groups in the United States, plus approximately the same number of college theatres, and perhaps 15,000 more groups in clubs, churches, schools, and even prisons.

In the late forties there were about a dozen movie houses— half of them in New York—that regularly showed so-called art films, foreign films, movie classics, and experimental shorts. Since then the audience for these has snowballed to the point at which today it supports an "art circuit" of some 500 theatres from Trenton, New Jersey, to Tempe, Arizona. The quality of films shown in the art circuit is uneven, and many "art houses" mix what the trade calls "exploitation films" in with their art. But the rise of the art film—most of its footage imported—is highly significant, coming, as it did, during a decade that saw over-all movie attendance drop from 60 million a week to 40 million.

Thousands of Americans are also quietly absorbing their culture at home. Witness the rise of FM radio stations, more than half of which are devoted almost entirely to broadcasting classical music, discussions of art, literature, and similar subjects.

There are today over 400 FM stations of this type with a large and faithful body of listeners. WFMT in Chicago, which doesn't hesitate to broadcast all four and a half hours of Wagner's *Parsifal* without interruption for commercials, in 1958 broke into the "Top Ten" list of Chicago stations as rated by the number of listeners. Today WFMT has a list of 25,000 subscribers who pay $5 a year for a monthly program guide that tells them when they can hear a performance of a suite by Telemann or a reading of T. S. Eliot's poetry.

Along with a new public interest have come changes in the relationship of the universities to the arts, in the basic attitudes of cultural institutions toward the public, and in the economic underpinning of the cultural machinery. Not only has there been a proliferation of college courses in art, music, drama, and kindred subjects, but since the end of the war hundreds of professional artists, musicians, poets, and sculptors have found their way onto college faculties. On many campuses now it is not uncommon to find a "resident artist" or a "resident composer." One of the most important results of this change has been to connect the campus with the cultural institutions of the surrounding community. Stanford Professor Sandor Salgo directs the Bach Festival in Carmel and the community orchestras of Marin County and San Jose. The famed Actor's Workshop in San Francisco was started by two members of the faculty of San Francisco State College, and in Los Angeles the faculty and graduates of the College of Fine Arts of UCLA have been responsible for sparking about a dozen community theatre groups. This interaction is even more evident in small cities. For example, the cultural bootstrap operation in Waterloo (pop.: 72,000) has been prodded along by State College of Iowa faculty members who staff the art course in the city-run recreation center and provide professional guidance for the Waterloo Symphony Orchestra, the choral association, and the chamber music organization.

Merchandising Culture

The cultural institutions themselves, in a radical turnabout in their basic posture toward the public, have become almost as "sales-minded" as business. Whereas before the war many had a take-it-or-leave-it attitude toward the public, today they are busily and consciously trying to create new "demand" for culture. The Metropolitan Opera Guild this year is presenting special performances of an abridged *Così Fan Tutte* in junior and senior high schools throughout the New York area. Symphonies have stepped up their special performances—pop concerts, suburban concerts, children's concerts. Libraries have multiplied the number of "bookmobiles," which extend lending facilities to remote districts.

The change in stance is most sharply evident in museums. Today art is being transported out of the museum buildings to places where larger numbers of people can enjoy them. The Dallas Museum of Fine Arts, for example, maintains a rotating collection of paintings in the busy terminal at Love Field. The Boston Museum of Fine Arts circulated 62,000 color slides to art clubs, individuals, and classes last year—about three times as many as ten years before. The Virginia Museum of Fine Arts in Richmond has been a leader in finding new ways to build the culture audience. It not only opened its doors at night for those who cannot conveniently visit the museum during the day, it put the world's first "artmobile" on the road, touring with a changing exhibition of paintings and sculpture.

Passing the Hat

It was almost inevitable, with the American penchant for organizing, that people would begin to coordinate all this activity. And so they have: "arts councils" have sprung up in many communities. Today there are more than forty cities in the United States, from Albany to Santa Barbara, in each of which the major local cultural organizations have banded together in loose federations. Some hundred other cities are considering organizing arts councils. How they work can be illustrated by the experience of the St. Paul Council of Arts and Sciences. In 1951 an interim committee formed from the Civic Opera Association, the Science Museum, a civic orchestra, the St. Paul Gallery and School of Art, and the Schubert Club (which brings touring musical artists to St. Paul) sat down to tackle certain problems they all shared. First, working closely with Frank Marzitelli, the city commissioner responsible for libraries, museums, and auditoriums, the group was successful in having a $1.7 million-bond-issue proposal included in an omnibus bond resolution placed before the voters in 1953. The $1.7 million was to pay for construction of a downtown arts and science center that would house the museum, concert and rehearsal facilities, gallery exhibition space, classrooms, and offices. In 1954 the interim committee dissolved and a permanent arts council was organized with a full-time director. It helps iron out scheduling conflicts among its affiliates, it maintains a master mailing list of seven thousand names, for all its groups, and it runs special membership drives for them. When St. Paul's orchestra group came to it for special assistance, the council helped devise a program that would supplement existing cultural activities rather than attempt to compete with the services of the first-class symphony orchestra in nearby Minneapolis. The St. Paul orchestra reconstituted itself on a nonprofessional basis; it set out to help create three local youth orchestras and it put on a series of educational-TV musical broadcasts.

But the most significant aspect of the council's work is its passing of the hat. The technique, used by arts councils in at least half a dozen cities, could remake the financial foundation of the arts in America. Most cultural organizations run deficits, and St. Paul's organizations were no exception. They would regularly conduct individual fund-raising campaigns, usually with amateurish enthusiasm but with wholly unprofessional methods. These campaigns netted the organizations in the St. Paul council a combined total of only $42,700 in 1958.

In 1959 the council, under its executive director, Ralph Burgard, launched a joint fund-raising drive, modeling its techniques after the familiar community-chest pattern. A central budget committee, which included a bank vice president, an accountant, an attorney, and the vice president of an insurance company, was created to screen the requests and the budgets of each of the affiliates. First, solicitors quietly visited the major donors of the past and began signing them up. A week before public solicitation began, the council mailed out thousands of copies of a brochure explaining the purposes of the drive; then about seven hundred volunteers began knocking on doors of friends and neighbors and businesses. When the drive was over, the council had chalked up $146,883 in contributions. The 1961 campaign target is $176,000.

The Corporate Maecenases

In Winston-Salem, which boasts one of the best and most active arts councils in the nation, businessmen have pitched enthusiastically into the job of joint fund raising for culture. Says one leader of the Winston-Salem council: "For years Western Electric, which employs more than eight thousand people down here, had not given a sou to the arts. Yet we found that the largest number of people at our cultural events were from the Western Electric Nike Zeus plant. So we went to them and told them we are providing a helluva lot of entertainment and personal advantages for their people, and we came away with a $2,000 contribution to the arts council. Western Electric came through again this year. A lot of industries won't give a cent to a single art. But they'll give if the arts are coordinated on a community basis."

Perhaps even more important, from a long-range standpoint, than the increasing amount of money being raised is the broadening of the base of art patronage. In 1958 the St. Paul council's member groups drew all of their contributions from only 320 individuals and businesses. By 1960 this number had grown to 3,200. In Louisville, 1950 contributions came from 1,200 donors, the 1960 total came from 6,000.

A still small, but growing, part of the new patronage is coming from business, as the St. Paul and Winston-Salem examples indicate. In Cincinnati, one of the first cities to apply the united-fund principle to cultural-fund raising, direct business contributions to the fund . . . increased from $225,000 in 1950 to $319,000 in 1961, and the number of individual donors from 4,535 to 19,449. Ninety companies in Cincinnati donated an average of $1.60 per employee. Thirty of them gave an average of $2.64 per employee.

Another increasing source of support for the arts is foundations, which gave about $34 million to the humanities last year. Usually their grants are intended as seed money to initiate a project or to stimulate the creation of new works, rather than to provide permanent operating funds.

Far more important, as of now, is the patronage bestowed by by cities and states. Most of this support goes to libraries and museums, long accepted as institutions needing public money.

Additional public funds flow into that part of the educational structure devoted to the arts. As the cultural audience has expanded, more and more cities and states are allocating funds to cultural activities that, some years ago, might have been considered outside the legitimate scope of public support. Thus last year Kentucky provided funds that enabled the Louisville Orchestra and the Louisville String Quartet to tour the state. The Kentucky State Division of Tourist and Travel Promotion is mounting art exhibits in state parks. Michigan recently created a state Cultural Commission to survey the state's artistic needs, and New York State, in a trail-blazing move, this year created a state arts council, with $450,000 to spend on the arts. Grants have been made to underwrite state tours of the City Center Opera Company, the New York City Ballet Company, the Phoenix Theatre, and the Buffalo Philharmonic Orchestra.

Dissemination or Dilution?

In sum, the character and quality of American society are being drastically changed, in both their public and private aspects, by mass interest in cultural activities. Perhaps this change is implied in the term "democratic civilization," a condition to which Americans seem to be moving and which is far broader than political democracy. The lack of historical precedent may be one reason that the present trend occasions so much disquiet and acrimonious debate in sophisticated quarters.

Good or bad, the trend is probably irreversible. A generation hence, interest in music, painting, books will probably be even more widespread than at present. By then, perhaps, we will know whether culture has been disseminated, as the optimists believe, or diluted, as the pessimists say. Meanwhile, a lot of Americans are enjoying their exposure to the arts, and many of them, surely, will develop appreciative faculties as sound as those that characterized the small critical elite of recent centuries.

PAPERBACKS: IT PAYS TO GO HIGH-BROW [2]

A decade and a half ago, if a teacher caught a schoolboy sneaking a paperback novel into class, chances are the pupil

[2] From article in *Business Week.* p 36-8. D. 30, '61. Reprinted by permission.

could resign himself to having the book confiscated, staying a half hour after school, or both. For paperback books meant sex, sadism, or the smoking gun—certainly not the classics.

Today, it's likely that the same teacher is regularly assigning four or five paperbacks to his class each semester as supplementary reading. Pocket Books, Inc., reports that two thirds of the 60 million books it sells in a year are bought by students. And the state of Texas has voted to spend $100,000 to look into the possibility of paperback textbooks for its public schools.

Such figures are evidence of the revolution that has come to the paperback book business. An entirely new market has been developed from practically nothing in twelve to fifteen years—mainly because paperback publishers are printing far better books than they did. This new market has been created without disturbing the growth rate of hard-cover books, library circulation, or hard-cover textbooks.

The soft-cover version of Leon Uris' *Exodus*, for example, was published while the hard-cover book was still No. 1 on best-seller lists. The hard-cover book continued to sell well, finishing at about 400,000 copies, a highly respectable figure. The paperback sold 4.5 million copies.

"It's impossible to estimate how many of these 4.5 million people would never have read the book—without a paperback edition available," says Oscar Dystel, president of Bantam Books, Inc., soft-cover publishers of *Exodus*.

Most publishers agree it's impossible to tell which came first, the new mass reading market or the new rush to print good literature in paperbacks. They note that even such admittedly high-brow paperbacks as George Orwell's *1984* (2 million copies) and Aldous Huxley's *Brave New World* (1.5 million) have run up remarkable sales totals.

But because the schools and the public have proved there's a mass market for good books, paperback publishers continue to upgrade their titles. In the last eighteen months alone, the number of titles of paperback books has doubled—from 6,500 to 13,900—mostly with books such as *Algeria in Turmoil*, by Michael K. Clark (Universal Library, a division of Grosset & Dunlap, Inc.); *Brahms, His Life and Work*, by Karl Geiringer (Anchor Books, a division of Doubleday & Company, Inc.); and *The Gathering Storm*, by Winston Churchill (Bantam).

"It's fantastic," says one New Jersey teacher. "No matter how obscure, no matter how specialized or academic, it seems that every significant book is now being published by someone in paperback."

Split Business

Paperback book publishers divide into two distinct types:

1. The mass-distribution field (such as Pocket Books, Bantam, New American Library), which sells its books to magazine wholesalers, who distribute them to 110,000 newsstands, drugstores, supermarkets. These books retail at fifty cents or seventy-five cents.

2. The limited-distribution field (such as Anchor; Universal Library; Vintage Books, published by Random House-Knopf; Grove Press, Inc.; and Meridian Books, published by World Publishing Company). This sells its books directly to 3,500 outlets, including 1,500 college bookstores and 300 all-paperback stores. These books, usually printed on heavier stock, retail at $1 to $3.

Both fields are growing fast. In the last five years, mass-distributed paperback sales have risen from 224 million units to 280 million, wholesale dollar volume from $41 million to $71 milion. Limited-distribution paperbacks sold 13 million copies in 1960, up from 10 million in 1959; wholesale volume jumped from under $3 million in 1955 to about $9.5 million in 1960.

The fundamental reasons for the sales climb, of course, are the low price of good books and the new market in schools and colleges ("The great majority of our books are bought by college students," says President Barney Rosset of Grove Press). But publishers add other explanations.

It's "the temper of the times," says President Manuel Siwek of Grosset & Dunlap. This "has created a fabulously greater interest in serious things. World crisis, scientific developments, the necessity of a college degree have each contributed."

The usual whipping boy, TV, gets a good word from Bantam's President Dystel. "Believe it or not," he says, "I think television is behind the whole thing. It has broadened people's horizons."

Movie tie-ins, though less related to the more serious books, sometimes play a part. Alistair MacLean's *Guns of Navarone* sold only 200,000 paperback copies in four years, then zoomed to 600,000 in three months after the movie came out.

Break-even Worries

It's not just a matter, of course, of sitting back and counting the cash that flows in. Because of varying cost structures and break-even points, the mass-distribution and limited-distribution publishers have different problems.

A publisher of higher-priced limited-distribution paperbacks can sell as few as 10,000 copies of each book and break even. Since these books are sold almost exclusively in bookstores and college bookshops, the publishers can put out highly technical or academic works and still be fairly sure of profitable sales.

The mass-distribution publisher, since his over-all margin is so low, must sell at least 150,000 copies of each book to break even. So he has to stick to works of a potentially more popular variety.

Recently, however, there has been a blurring of the dividing lines, with some mass-distribution people publishing a higher-priced line for bookstores, and some limited-distribution publishers bringing out a lower-priced line for newsstands.

One fairly recent development has tended to push the mass distributor's break-even point even higher. That's the increase in the reprint rights payment—what amounts to a lump-sum royalty guarantee paid by paperback houses to original hard-cover publishers.

Fawcett Publications, Inc., for example, won reprint rights to William L. Shirer's *The Rise and Fall of the Third Reich* (Simon & Schuster, Inc.) with a bid of $400,000. Fawcett is reluctant to estimate, but other publishers say the break-even point will be over 2 million copies—nearly as much as the soft-cover sales of the very popular *Hawaii*, by James A. Michener. . . .

Some paperback publishers, trying to reverse the trend and cut their costs, are buying manuscripts and farming them out for hard-cover "preprints."

Glutted Market?

The paperback idea—reprint or original—is, of course, not new. Its U.S. ancestors were the dime novel, the popular library, and pulp fiction. The first successful U.S. paperback reprint venture of the current era began with the founding of Pocket Books in 1939. In Europe, the first big success came with Tauchnitz, founded in Germany in 1837. In 1930, Tauchnitz found itself with a British competitor, Penguin.

Today, there are eighteen U.S. publishers in the mass-distribution field, putting out 185 titles a month—against eighty-two for the field seven years ago. Almost every hard-cover publisher has a limited-distribution paperback line. Many previously hesitant are jumping in full force. Crowell-Collier Publishing Company alone is publishing fifty new titles a month. The Macmillan Company, McGraw-Hill Publishing Company, Inc., and others are developing paperback textbooks.

Consequently, some established publishers worry about a glutted market—yet sales figures remain high. All-paperback bookshops are opening all over the country. Considering that the school population will grow by some 45 per cent in five years and the number of Americans who have finished high school is almost 150 per cent greater than ten years ago, there seems little reason for the paperback market to falter.

MASS COMMUNICATIONS: "LITERATE" MAGAZINES [3]

For some time now there has been considerable comment heralding the "cultural explosion" that supposedly is sweeping the land. In the magazine industry, however, this talk has been taken with a grain of salt. Publishers note, for example, that the supposed "explosion" has not had any particularly explosive effect upon the circulations of most of the nation's leading cultural magazines.

Though some of these magazines have made notable gains, some others have remained on circulation plateaus.

The situation confronting the American Heritage Publishing Company is a good example. Five years ago, the company started a general cultural magazine called *Horizon*, and the hard-cover monthly soon achieved a circulation of about 150,000.

But the magazine has been unable to surpass that point—indeed *Horizon's* circulation now has tumbled to about 129,000.

[3] From "Advertising: Cultural Magazines on Plateau," by Peter Bart, New York *Times* correspondent. New York *Times*. p 44. S. 6, '63. © 1963 by The New York Times Company. Reprinted by permission.

The magazine has had two profitable years and three unprofitable ones.

Yesterday, *Horizon* announced some changes that were designed to get it off its plateau. The regular annual subscription price will be reduced from $21 to $16 with a special introductory price of $12.95 and a renewal price of $12.75. In addition, the magazine will be published quarterly rather than monthly.

The changes will not affect the company's other periodical, *American Heritage*, which is published twice a month. *American Heritage*'s most recent report showed a circulation of 294,000, slightly below its 300,000 average of the last five years.

Other "literate" magazines have had varying degrees of success in recent years, with some showing sharp gains and others only modest ones. The circulation of *The Reporter* has increased from 121,013 to 173,769; *Harper's* from 190,850 to 282,000; *The Atlantic* from 258,097 to 270,000; *Saturday Review* from 156,190 to 317,126; *Esquire* from 812,000 to 883,815; *Commentary* from 19,000 to 32,000, and *The Nation* from 24,000 to 30,000.

MASS COMMUNICATIONS: THE PRESS COVERS CULTURE[4]

When the New York *Times* appointed a "Director of Cultural News" two years ago, a collective shudder ran down the spines of newspaper veterans. What, they inquired, was the business coming to? They turned the phrases "culture beat" and "culture editor" over in their mouths with the gusto of a man biting into an unripe olive.

If he had not been a cultured man, the new Director of Cultural News at the *Times*, Joseph Herzberg, might have experienced a twinge or two himself. Herzberg had been a noted news executive on the *Herald Tribune* for many years. He had come to the *Times* as assistant city editor, specializing in the development of investigative news stories, until the day he was transplanted from the familiar rhythm of the city room to a large department, with its own copy desk, where fifty people under his direction were devoting themselves to reporting manifestations of that abused word "culture."

[4] From "Newspapers and the Culture Beat," by John Tebbel, author and chairman of the department of journalism, New York University. *Saturday Review.* 46:61+. Ap. 13, '63. Reprinted by permission.

Despite the doubters, Herzberg and the *Times* knew what they were doing. They were treating the growing cultural activities of Americans as news, and today there is a trend among the best dailies to do likewise. In their various ways, they are making an attempt to deal with the results of what is still resolutely called "the cultural explosion," a phrase that makes most writers and editors wince. . . .

The newspapers are responding to this growth in several ways. Some, with limited staffs and only a cautious enthusiasm, are doing no more than giving a little extra Sunday space to culture. Others are printing more daily and Sunday book reviews. Some of the leaders are not only increasing daily coverage, but are expanding Sunday sections and trying to edit them in a more imaginative way. Often these moves have been made without a direct relation to advertising revenue, the usual motive for increased specialized coverage. In these days of critical cost problems, this requires the courage of a publisher's convictions.

One of the most striking of the new Sunday or weekend productions is "Panorama," published on Saturdays by the Chicago *Daily News* and launched this year. It is a result of the conviction shared by publisher Marshall Field, Jr., and executive editor Larry Fanning that culture is as much news in Chicago as elsewhere.

Chicago has had for many years one of the best book reviewing media in the country in the *Tribune's* "Sunday Magazine of Books," but "Panorama" is something new. It is frankly intellectual, and it is comprehensive in its coverage of the arts in and out of Chicago, including a guide to theatre, music, exhibits, films, special events, and lectures.

For anyone concerned about the state of midwestern culture, a recent issue of "Panorama" guide listed eight professional, three college, five community, and five "revue" productions currently on the boards. (In the old days "revue" meant burlesque; today it means social satire of the kind which made *Second City* a New York hit after it left Chicago.) Along with these productions, the music section listed, among other offerings, Chicago Symphony Orchestra concerts; a program by the Fine Arts Quartet; a new work of the contemporary composer Pierre Boulez, played by a chamber ensemble; two dance recitals; opera at

Northwestern University; and visiting dancers and musicians from North India.

"Panorama" offers big names on the culture beat. In recent issues Chicagoans could read Stephen Spender on "Why I Am a Poet," Robert M. Hutchins on "What Is Education?" and Hyman G. Rickover on "Freedom Is the Answer." One issue alone contained the Spender piece, two views of Adenauer, a poem about Carl Sandburg, an article about motion pictures by the curator of films of the Museum of Modern Art in New York, an excerpt from a longer *American Heritage* piece by J. H. Plumb about George III, two pages of book reviews, two pages of art news and reviews, a music page, record reviews, and features on local amusements about town.

All this is a long way from the culture coverage of yesterday, when city editors often sent unlettered reporters to cover music and art events with instructions to report them simply as straight news, inasmuch as they were not qualified critics. Motion picture reviews on many papers were publicity handouts from the exhibitors, and books were often not reviewed at all.

The argument for such limp coverage was that public interest did not call for anything more, space was too hard to come by, and in any case there was not enough advertising to support it. Space is still a difficult problem and advertising for the arts is not in proportion to the volume of news (a twenty-four-page issue of "Panorama" carries only twelve pages on which advertising appears), but the public interest has increased to the point where a substantial number of newspapers have had to pay attention.

Culture, indeed, is now a matter of local pride. Citizens boast about their art museums and symphony orchestras as well as their sports teams. Louisville, Kentucky, stung a decade or more ago by a national magazine's reference to it as "a cultural desert," has so rehabilitated itself through the efforts of citizens' committees that "the people can hardly stand it," in the jocular words of one who helped bring about the transformation. The Louisville *Courier-Journal's* extensive coverage of the arts has been a major help here.

The idea of culture as news beyond the mere reporting of events, or even the reviewing of them, is being accepted by a good many newspapers. Books offer the best news opportunities because they are controversial on occasion and thus provide news stories off the book page. Promotion and publicity people in publishing houses think such stories help sell books because they enlist the attention of people who would not ordinarily read reviews. Whether such people ever buy books is another of those unanswered questions which plague publishing, an industry that spends almost nothing for research.

The book industry itself is news, but it has never been reported adequately by any New York newspaper, in the city where it is centered. Most have not reported it at all. The *Times* hopes to be the first to do so by having a reporter full time in its cuture department to cover the industry as a beat.

Whatever the merits of that argument, there is no question that the culture beat, in whatever struggling form it may be emerging, has added a new dimension to American newspapering which is both welcome and needed.

ATTENDANCE SOARS AT MUSEUMS [5]

Winds of innovation, sometimes blowing at gale force, are whistling through the vaulted halls of America's museums.

They are driving "Indian arrowheads in serried ranks assembled" into deep storage and infusing museum exhibits with light, color, sound and prudent animation. Once-dusty repositories for plaster casts of Winged Victory are coming alive with invention.

The lines on attendance graphs, sloping steadily upward since World War II, are rising more steeply. Curators speak boldly of a "renaissance" of a popular appreciation of the arts.

The number of museums in the nation is increasing by what seems an endless series of jumps of two's and three's. In New York State there were fewer than 200 museums in 1931. There are more than 400 now.

In small cities, museums are serving as the focus of every cultural activity. To house the lively and the classic arts, many small cities have little but motion-picture theatres. There, museums are providing refuges for artists in every other form.

[5] From "Attendance Soars at Museums Here," by McCandlish Phillips, New York *Times* correspondent. New York *Times*. p 1+. N. 27, '61. © 1961 by The New York Times Company. Reprinted by permission.

In New York City, museums are on the brink of considerable expansion. Silver spades have already turned some earth and will soon put ceremonial dents in more.

In display improvements, the best is soon to come. On the desks, in the closets or framed in the minds of museum directors are sketches, scale models and minutely detailed dreams. These are designed to put trustees in a mood to spend.

The Metropolitan Museum of Art was having a triumphant year at its entrances before it opened the money sluices and spent $2.3 million at auction for Rembrandt's "Aristotle Contemplating the Bust of Homer."

86,770 for Metropolitan

Dazzled by so grand a sum, and eager to judge for themselves if the painting is worth the price of a missile, 86,770 persons pressed into the museum in four hours. . . .

With 3,311,400 visitors . . . the Metropolitan . . . [was] already way over its record of 3,017,309 visitors in 1959, with five weeks to go.

The American Museum of Natural History had 2,041,000 visitors . . . [in 1960], putting it above 2,000,000 for the first time since 1952. In the fiscal year ending . . . June 30 [1962], it hoped to touch 3,000,000. These figures do not include an annual count of 600,000 at the Hayden Planetarium.

The Brooklyn Museum, full of signs of new vitality, shot up from 418,300 visitors in 1959 to 529,400 in 1960 and is still scoring gains. Other museums here are having very good or even boom years.

Rising attendance figures and new ways to tempt lookers to become members have swelled museum rolls this year. Museum publishing activities have also prospered.

Leisure a Factor

Museum executives attribute the popularity of museums to the following influences, among others:

Increased money and leisure to devote to an interest in the arts.

A public cultivated to a new consciousness of styles, periods and modes, again a product of leisure time.

The coming of age of a generation that became attached to museums when young because of the museums' intensive programs of child education.

Space given to museum attractions by newspapers, magazines and television, but notably by *Life*, whose full-color spreads have conveyed excitement to many.

The attractiveness, timeliness and genius of museum displays, some of which are tied to headlines.

Renaissance Seen

There are directors who believe the museums are experiencing symptoms of a popular cultural renaissance. And they dare to think that this may so amply feed secret springs of human creativity as to burst into a quite majestic fountain.

A cultural renaissance is occurring in this country, there is no question about it [James V. Noble, operating administrator, said at the Metropolitan].

In ancient Greece, citizens were expected to play musical instruments, to be politically aware, to be creative enough to sing—not just convivial songs—to read the ancient authors, to write poetry and to recite it meaningfully. I see this very thing occurring here. . . .

It is necessary, Mr. Noble said, to have a broad popular "groundswell before the heights are reached, the surge you get in periods of greatness." . . .

Upsurge in Art Books

Women wearing cloth coats pluck large, expensive, richly illustrated art books off the shelves of bookstores or museum gift shops almost as casually as they take cheese from a supermarket display.

The art book market, once a specialized service for the privileged or indulgent few, has become a tremendously profitable mass market.

Ralph R. Miller, director of the Museum of the City of New York, said that if one were to plot a curve of the public's affection for museums "it would break sharply up since the last war." He continued:

Twenty-five or thirty years ago, if you said to someone, "I am going to work in a museum," they would say, "Are they going to embalm you, or what?" Now a very dynamic program is in evidence in museums all over the country. I think, hopefully, we are completely out of the embalmed-mummy category.

Maybe we are in the ascendancy and approaching a renaissance of museums in the social life of America.

"We have begun to create a whole new generation of people who are aware of the importance of the arts," an officer at the Museum of Modern Art said, speaking of educational activities.

The crops of children have been growing up in an art-oriented atmosphere, and now they are bringing their children in [an executive at the Metropolitan noted]. One of the most frequent complaints we get is from young mothers who don't understand why they can't wheel their baby coaches through the galleries.

I saw a baby in a little bassinette checked at the counter at the National Museum in Washington.

Weekday museum attendance figures include a high proportion of school children, mostly in groups that come by appointment for tours or classes. But it is very easy for adults to sidestep these coveys.

Lone small children in museums on weekdays are often rudely surprised by school attendance officers, who roam the galleries collaring truants.

Week Ends Frantic

On week ends the Great Hall at the Metropolitan is about as busy as Grand Central Terminal, and traffic in and out of the chambers of the Tomb of Per-Neb is so heavy that a viewer can scarcely pause to study the intricately figured interior.

An officer at the Museum of Modern Art said: "On week ends it can get so crowded it's miserable."

On the other hand, the larger museums are often lonely places on weekdays, and one can tour their tranquil halls like the master of some princely palace filled with the rare and wonderful.

Executives at the Metropolitan are not sure whether to laugh or to weep over their great favor with the public.

"It presents us with very many problems," James J. Rorimer, the director, said. He described women's spike heels as "my *bête noire.*"

Unapproachable Sphinx

"People ask us why we keep our rose granite sphinx in the Great Hall chained off. We do it to keep him from being patted to death," Mr. Noble said.

On the other hand, the Museum of the City of New York has a "Please Touch Room," in which children are invited to handle displays.

And there is no museum that so gladly suffers nose marks and finger smudges as the American Museum of [Natural History]—the "Dinosaur Museum" to generations of little boys.

We have a terrible problem with chewing gum and melting ice cream sticks [Dr. James A. Oliver, the director, said]. We don't sell any ice cream on sticks inside, but in the summer Good Humor men seem to surround the museum.

But this place is a wonderland for kids, and it's the gateway to science for many youngsters.

We've had a number of kids that came round here, kept asking questions and made a nuisance of themselves by their omnipresence and, happily, have gone on to become scientists.

Dr. Richard G. Van Gelder began hanging around here as a kid. Now he's chairman of our mammology department. And he isn't the only case.

Arthur Drexler, the young director of architecture and design at the Museum of Modern Art, haunted the museum as a high school student.

These are two of the trophies of "the museum-oriented generation."

Children in Confusion

Four days of looking at people looking at museums disclosed that children, except those under tight rein, explore museums with little fixity of purpose.

In the Brooklyn Museum, two boys, dragging their windbreakers on the stone floor, cruised among the gods of Ancient Egypt, going from case to case without a pause, as though under some obligation to come into momentary proximity to everything.

Children were seen "doing" huge halls, half the size of cathedrals, in ninety seconds, their eyes not coming to rest for more than three seconds on any object. Man has strewn the world with pottery for milleniums, but what children seem to seek is action.

Fortunately, supervised activities for children are preponderant. The Brooklyn Museum's first-floor classrooms are noise- and child-filled most afternoons. Every Monday and Tuesday 975 children flock in for concerts.

At the American Museum, Dr. Oliver said that although the museum was taking in two thousand young visitors daily, it was also obliged to "turn away" one thousand children a day because of a lack of classrooms and instructors.

A Weeding-Out

There was a time when museum halls were heavy with somber antiquity. Rows of objects were often tightly jammed into cases, take them or leave them.

Now, more and more, imagination and selectivity and drama go into their presentation.

Lavishness and a flair for showmanship are amply illustrated in the American Museum's plan to use, as the centerpiece of its new Hall of Ocean Life, an eighty-foot whale made of fiberglas.

When the hall is opened in 1964, the whale will be shown beached, lying on its side as though stranded on Fire Island. Lights will play slowly over its surface to represent sun and shadow. Visitors will hear the sound of the surf and the call of sea birds.

Art museums are, perforce, rather less expansive in their innovations.

An exception to this may be the Solomon R. Guggenheim Museum, which is in itself an innovation. It was designed by the late Frank Lloyd Wright to provide a continuous spiral gallery rising on a ramp from the base to the dome of a circular structure. The museum was opened in 1959.

The Museum of Modern Art enjoys a remarkable degree of freedom in arranging its displays. The large gallery floors have, of course, permanent shells, but interior walls are redesigned for each new exhibition. The museum is planning a new wing, to open early in 1964, affording, if possible, an even more flexible interior by the use of clear-span construction.

For a one-man show of sculpture, woodcuts, drawings and other works by Bernard Reder this fall, the Whitney Museum of American Art was obedient to Mr. Reder's strong conviction that sculpture should be seen in the round.

The argument was that sculpture, unlike painting, is meant to be seen from every possible angle, since the sculptor invests as much in the back of a piece as in the front. A niche is the worst place for a sculptured figure, Mr. Reder says.

We built a very elaborate two-branched ramp, whose height varied from floor level to four feet [the Whitney associate director, John Baur, explained].

The pieces were spotted among the curves of the ramps, providing an infinite variety of heights from which to observe them. With "The Wounded Woman," which is three feet high, you get an aerial view and an entirely different appreciation of the relationship of the several figures in the composition.

At the Metropolitan, Mr. Rorimer said:

People hadn't looked at Chinese vases for a generation. It's been thought they were out of fashion. I insisted it wasn't the fashion but the way they were shown. We proved it by changing the installation on our Altman Collection of Chinese porcelains.

Though the collection includes vases of exquisite symmetry, the public had paid them little attention for years. Then the ceiling was lowered and the porcelains were more sparingly and stylishly arranged under bountiful lighting behind white glass (most glass is faintly green). They are now receiving careful attention.

Mr. Rorimer said he planned thus to simplify and beautify many collections at the Metropolitan.

He has been working on a plan to construct "inner and outer circuits" in, typically, a gallery of Greek vases. Partitions would afford a central corridor through the gallery in which about thirty of the finest specimens would be displayed for the casual visitor.

For the expert, the student and the very curious, seven hundred more vases would be shown beyond the partitions.

Under Thomas S. Buechner, its thirty-five-year-old director, the Brooklyn Museum plans a revolution to do away with the "iceberg" character common to collections in many museums, by which a majority of all possessions are either not readily visible or are inaccessible in "dead storage."

Mr. Buechner hopes, within five years, to bring every last item of the Brooklyn Museum's holdings out of storage.

He believes the museum now shows too many items for the general visitor and too few for the specialized or expert visitor.

Under the plan, limited selections of major pieces would be placed on primary display. Everything else would be accessible in a "very unpretentious sort of open storeroom" to which the visitor would be admitted on request.

A related plan is to "make some of the more exciting activities of the museum staff visible to the public" by the installation of glass walls.

The public would be able to watch the pigment and binder of an old painting being transferred from "an evil support" to a strong new canvas.

Dr. Oliver at the American Museum said he thought that doing "a better job of interpreting exhibits" was the "area of great challenge as far as public service is concerned."

Ideally, every museum visitor would be accompanied by an urbane and knowledgeable guide, preferably one who would speak only when spoken to.

Since this is impossible, directors are turning to mechanical devices. Even the staid Metropolitan hopes soon to be wired for sound.

In late July, what was described as "the world's first bilingual, three-channel radio guide service" was installed in ten of the American Museum's fifty-eight halls.

A visitor who rents a receiver for fifty cents a day may hear a five-minute résumé in English or Spanish of what is in each of the ten halls, and he may hear a fifteen-minute talk in English by the curator in charge. A visitor does best to move thorugh the hall as the narrator directs.

The museum hopes to expand this Soundtrek system, developed at Dr. Oliver's suggestion, at the rate of three or four halls a year. It also intends to use movies "more and more" to supplement exhibits.

The Metropolitan thinks that its sound system, now in development, will be the best available anywhere.

The visitor will not be obliged to move at the pace of the narration. If he wishes to pause to examine an object, he will be able to switch the narration off without losing any of it.

The museum hopes to have the first [segment] of the system ready in a few months. Experimental tapes are now being prepared. The tapes may include a general tour of the highlights of the entire museum as well as gallery talks.

The Brooklyn Museum is now working on a sound service.

The Museum of the City of New York has found that its "walking tours," in which distinguished raconteurs lead a party among city landmarks, are a powerful means of recruiting members. Ten per cent of those who take the tours join the museum, and this is regarded as "a very good yield."

Mr. Rorimer said that the purchase of the Rembrandt had already given the Metropolitan's membership rolls a gratifying increase. The Metropolitan has about 16,000 members, while the Museum of Modern Art, which has been "cultivating membership pretty assiduously," has 30,000.

The Whitney Museum, which had inadequate acquisition funds in 1954, formed an organization called Friends of the Whitney with annual dues of $250. This has "added greatly" to its ability to purchase new works.

ART MERCHANDISING [6]

Mass merchandising of fine art is a contradiction in something deeper than terms, but the experiment is being carried on by Sears, Roebuck & Co. just now in its Brooklyn store, and also in its Huntington, Long Island, branch. With Vincent Price as its combination buyer, salesman-in-absentia and commentator, the experiment is less revolutionary than it sounds. It is an extension to a mass public of principles that have applied to fine art and a somewhat more limited public for many years now.

Anyone interested in seeing just how this works need only go to the furniture department in the Brooklyn store where temporary screens have been set up alongside beds and cribs to hold original works of art in a price range beginning at $30 and going to nearly $10,000. It is a cheek-by-jowl display of original paintings, drawings and prints that have the single common denominator of Mr. Price's approval.

[6] From "Merchandising of Art Is Not Really Revolutionary," by John Canaday, New York *Times* art critic. New York *Times*. p 28. My. 24, '63. © 1963 by The New York Times Company. Reprinted by permission.

Sears has always done and still does an immense business in framed reproductions, ranging from the "Mona Lisa" all the way down, many of them at prices greater than those of some of the originals now for sale. A couple of years ago the company commissioned Mr. Price to start the project. As a collector and a public figure of some glamour already associated with art and culture in the public mind, Mr. Price was the perfect choice.

He set about purchasing art in wholesale quantities, buying entire collections when he could find them, clearing out the storerooms of dealers who had been letting good but not currently popular artists gather dust and, on a less wholesale basis, buying from little-known artists in whom he had faith and adding such fillips as original Légers and Vlamincks.

In Brooklyn a Léger gouache and a Vlaminck oil at prices above $6,000 and $8,000 hang around the corner from nineteenth century engravings at $35, in an unorganized line-up of about a hundred other items. As an exhibition, the display has no scheme; the pictures are simply hung for display, accompanied by price tags and a typed paper with Mr. Price's interpretative comments and explanations.

Prices are about the market average in most cases. Insofar as bargains are offered, they are less a matter of good things at unusually low prices than of good things that have been underpriced for some time and to which Mr. Price calls attention. Whistler etchings at less than $50 have long been available if you are not fussy about rarity and quality of impression. By digging these out in some quantity, Mr. Price has probably made them more expensive on the market, but in the meanwhile those offered for sale go off Sears's walls immediately. With Whistler and Vincent Price both as guarantees, what more do you want?

Sales slips indicate that items between $30 and $200 went fastest. While I was looking at the slips a woman purchased a Hogarth engraving for $60 and a Millet etching for, I think, $80, including frames. They could have been purchased at many places at the same prices or, with much looking, could have been found at lower prices. Mr. Price's contribution is in making such items conveniently available—so available that you can take them right out of the show and carry them home. . . .

People who buy these originals at Sears range from New York dealers to drop-ins who don't know an etching from an oil painting but whose faith in Mr. Price's preselection predisposes them in favor of something guaranteed to be genuine art. The extreme range of subject and treatment, from sentimental Victorian engravings to contemporary abstractions, offers something for everybody in this quality-guaranteed bazaar. If the element of predigestion is bothersome, we must remember that in a narrower range many a collector depends on the taste-making of less democratic figures than Mr. Price, and in some cases takes more of a chance.

MASS CULTURE/POPULAR CULTURE [7]

Thinking about mass culture these days, we seem increasingly to want to take a second or third or fourth step before we have taken the first. Or so I think a careful study of our essays and studies shows. Perhaps we fear that that first step is a step backward. And so it is—into ourselves. For once we admit something so overwhelmingly simple as the fact that we must live together in our community, we shall be obliged to inquire into what Edward Sapir long ago taught us to call the genuineness of spuriousness of our culture: that which gives our community such wholeness as it has. We say that our culture, any culture, is genuine to the degree that it allows full play to our sense of the dignity of man, spurious to the degree that it narrows or distorts or inhibits that sense. Hence we can do no less than begin at the beginning, within ourselves in our community, however narrow, distorted, or inhibited we may be. But it has been ever thus in the humanistic studies. . . .

Thus I think that a good deal of the contemporary debate about mass (or popular) culture is beside the point. Opponents in the debate have accepted—too soon I think—somewhat simplified versions of the historical situation which has made for mass culture and then gone on to show how the products of mass culture demonstrate the horror or the glory of the historical situation.

[7] From "Mass Culture/Popular Culture: Notes for a Humanist's Primer," by Roy Harvey Pearce, author, professor of English, and chairman of the department of literature at the University of California, San Diego. *College English.* 23:417-32. Mr. '62. Reprinted with the permission of the National Council of Teachers of English and Roy Harvey Pearce.

If history evidences progress, mass culture must somehow be a "good" thing: if it evidences regress, mass culture must somehow be a "bad" thing. To show that it is good, you point out how many good LP's, good paperbacks, good prints are selling and you bring up the fact of our museums-without-walls. To show that it is bad, you point out how much trash we are exposed to, how the purchase of good LP's and the like may be simply marks of longing for status; and you bring up the fact that in the museum-without-walls the great painting, cut down to its viewer's size, may function merely as a decorative plaque, part of the wallpaper. And of course, both sides of the debate are right in so far as their evidence is concerned. Strangely enough, they often interpret a given piece of evidence identically and then proceed to evaluate it in diametrically opposed fashions —according to their progressive or regressive theories of history. The debaters (they are lined up neatly in the Rosenberg-White *Mass Culture* volume and the Spring 1960 issue of *Daedalus*) are not really quarreling with each other; they are quarreling with history—with the fact that they, like the rest of us, have been born into this world. The net result is the fact that nearly everyone is now his own mass medium; that writing about mass culture has become a form of mass culture; and that whereas we may well be satisfied by a given writer's account of the intrinsic nature and quality of a given item of mass culture, we may well be dissatisfied with his account of the implication of that nature and quality for our quite concrete and specific existential problem: What is mass culture to us and what are we to mass culture? The problem, I suggest, is one of attaining a perspective that will not allow us to escape the fact that, like it or not, we have to *live* with mass culture. We must take our history straight. Which is to say, take ourselves in our history straight.

How, in the midst of the mass of mass culture, bowed down by its weight, seeing the hopes for a popular culture increasingly frustrated, how are we to know, judge, and discriminate? How are we to establish the means whereby such knowledge, judgment, and discrimination might not only preserve and inculcate the idea of a popular culture, but advance it?

My suggestions are humanistic, therefore academic. They consist essentially in learning how to think of mass as against popular culture, then—and only then—to act as one can. In these notes I am concerned to set down some necessary conditions of the act.

1. HISTORICALLY. . . . We will observe, I think, that even at its best popular culture is a peculiarly historistic thing—by which I mean to say that it is not intended to survive the lifetime of its immediate audience, or the phase-of-sensibility of its immediate audience. It gets used up, consumed, but it need not thereby be poisonous. Too, we will observe, of course, that in the nature of the increasing technification of the media, in the development of the mass media themselves—the possibility of such responsibility becomes increasingly difficult of realization. Careful, objective historical studies—sympathetic where sympathy is deserved—will at least sharpen and deepen our sense of the qualitative criteria of popular (as against mass) culture.

2. SOCIOLOGICALLY. (I use the term in the sense of what Wright Mills calls "the sociological imagination"—which "enables its possessor to understand the larger historical scene in terms of its meaning for the inner life and the external career of a variety of individuals." For Mills "history" is essentially contemporary history—the way we categorize and comprehend our lives now, our experience, in our milieu as a somehow coherent complex of lived-through events.) The problem here is to isolate for study the relation of mass culture as produced and consumed (horrible words!) to the socio-political structure and function of our society. What is it, we ask, to be a mass consumer? And inevitably our gaze is drawn hypnotically to the young—for whom the mass media have not only transformed a life style but have created one. Their character is one which is in great part fixed by the fact that everything—information, material goods, means of having fun, even the monuments of elite culture— seem to be available with the minimum effort on their part. They grow up very fast—having in high school worked through all the "activities" which used to be in the purview of college. They are trained to be consumers—their only consumer's guide the radio-TV segments which give the show a reason for going on. Their world view is fatefully conditioned by the idea of automation and of simultaneity of communication. Everything seems to happen, perhaps does happen, at once—yet the happenings are fragmented and the center will not hold. Perhaps there *is* no center, just a homogenized whole. Young people, as Paul

Goodman says, grow up "absurd." Their need is to *fill* all the free time they have, not to *use* it; and their need is confirmed and deepened by the cultural fare they are offered. They become mistrustful of information as such, of words, of gestures, of ideas: all of which imply a central cultural style which they cannot sense. Unhappily: the more "insightful" among them are cynical, or at best disenchanted, about the possibility of a popular, as opposed to a mass, culture—about a popular, as opposed to a mass, education. They are so cynical that they don't bother to confront squarely the fact that their world has been transformed once and for all, irreversibly, into one in which the mass media, automation, and the like have freed them from some of the discontents of work. Surely their obligation is also to live in the world, even in that part of it we would teach them to earn the right to despise; they can't earn the right to despise it by disaffiliating from it. One way of living in the world, so even this sociological critique would seem to demonstrate, is to learn to think intelligently and critically about mass culture and to learn to differentiate it from popular culture.

3. FORMALLY. The problem here is one for the "critic," and involves his usual compulsion to see the relation of form to content. He studies an item of popular culture. Is this a daydream, he asks, or a nightmare? Is it held in proper check, psychically contained, by its form? Is it related to reality? Or does the form serve only to make it a substitute for reality? (Here, of course, "reality" is the first term of Freud's "reality-principle": what is, in the nature of man and his world, humanly possible of achievement.) What portion of reality does it deal with and how? What are the characteristics of its medium and what problems do these characteristics pose for the popular artist who would to his reality principle be true? What is the conception of human nature upon which the operation of the medium is postulated? And then follows a question as to the relation of particular forms as used in mass (or popular) culture and their use in elite culture: the question of course, of what is called *kitsch* [artistic or literary material of low quality]. Critics have more and more observed how the objects of elite art are imitated in mass culture, and in the imitating drained of their integral value and import. Corollary to this is the fact that objects of folk art too have been imitated thus—from folklore to

fakelore, as the saying goes. Certainly, it is true that only the inauthentic—mass culture at its most vicious—is produced when an object of mass culture is offered as an easily earned surrogate for an object of elite or of folk culture. But I am not convinced entirely that the intelligent borrowing of forms and motifs from elite and folk art is necessarily vicious. After all, the wonderful popular songs of the seventeenth century take much of their strength from the folk songs which inspire them; and this is true in our own time too. There is clearly a descending line from the performance of a Mississippi chain gang to that of The Weavers to that of The Kingston Trio. Yet the performance of the latter still is not necessarily offered as a substitute for the performance of the former, but, as it were, only as an introduction to it. And there might well be an *ascending* line. From rock 'n' roll to Washboard Sam and the country blues—who knows? The point is that the possibility of moving from a popular to a folk form is not foreclosed. In its not being foreclosed—this is perhaps the proper relation of popular art to folk art; and I should think something comparable holds for the relation of popular art to elite art: *My Fair Lady* to *Pygmalion;* advertising layout to Mondrian; Paddy Chayefsky to Chekhov; Ted Williams to Nick Adams. When the possibility of moving from a popular to a folk or elite form is foreclosed, when there is no vital relation between the one and the other, then we have mass art for the mass consumer—not popular art for the popular auditor or reader or singer or whistler or whatever.

I think that just as the shift from a painting by Kandinsky, to a monumental building by Gropius, to a Tech-Built house is evidence of a vital relation between elite and popular art, so such a relation exists (and can exist) for our songs and stories. The relationship is possible, however, only if conditions are such as to let the maker's sense of responsibility to his audience predominate. Indeed, in the formal analysis of popular as well as of folk and elite art, what we mean when we speak of form or style, is the maker's means of being responsible in and for the portion of reality which his work comprehends. Some words of the great Finnish architect Alvar Aalto on the problem of mass housing today are relevant here:

Standardization . . . does not mean a formal one with all houses built alike. Standardization will be used mainly as a method of producing a flexible system by which the single house can be made adjustable for families of different sizes, various topographical locations, different exposures, views, etc.

Popular culture, considered formally, must be "standardized," so that through technology it can be made readily available to the popular audience. But, within the limits of its audience's sensibility, it can be made adjustable—so as to let members of the audience relax, refresh themselves, and simply enjoy the fact that what they have in common is the fact that they are different: their humanity half engaged. And I should say that it is the corollary function of elite art to urge its audience to commitment, meditation in depth, so as to contemplate the fact—so "real" as to be beyond enjoyment—that what makes its members different is what they have in common: their humanity *fully* engaged. Mass culture, of course, is humanity *dis*engaged, atrophying—form exhausting content, content eating cancerously at form. It is predicated upon the existence of a world in which our central problem—holding together our images of the world we have and the one we ought to have—in which this problem is as irrelevant as are those of us who would think about it. We intellectuals don't understand the mass audience, so proclaims Dr. Frank Stanton of CBS—and I am here paraphrasing some words of his published in the mass-culture issue of *Daedalus*. [See "Parallel Paths," Section IV, below.] We are given part of CBS's time: so we should let the masses enjoy themselves. What Dr. Stanton doesn't understand is that willy-nilly we are part of the mass audience too. Only, being intellectuals, we know the difference between a mass and a public, a crowd and community, between aspirin and that stuff Dr. Stanton's clients would overcharge us for—the overcharge being our ticket of admission to Madison-Avenue-produced entertainments whose aim is to convince us that it is worth while being overcharged: proof positive of the value of the American way of life; brain tinting out of the laboratories of Helena Rubenstein. Happily, there are a few (not many, but a few) self-parodists in the mass arts who know, or seem to know, the difference too—for example, he who creates Pogo; he who publishes *Mad;* and he who recorded a couple of years ago chipmunk voices which are like Fabian's and Frankie Avalon's—only more so.

Thus my three perspectives: *historical, sociological, formal.* It is obvious that each is a version of the other; and that the major student of mass and popular culture—he to whom we shall have to go to school—will work from all three perspectives at once and so discover the complexities of his humanism. The nearest things we have to inclusive studies of the sort I envisage are Raymond Williams' *Culture and Society* and his *Long Revolution,* Richard Hoggart's *Uses of Literacy,* Father William Lynch's *Image Industries,* Reuel Denney's *Astonished Muse,* and Gilbert Seldes' *The Popular Arts;* and all these are weakened, I think, by a curious foreshortening of their historical perspective. But they are powerful books; and I think that all humanists should come to know them. Their attitude toward the popular audience (with which their authors are quite willing to identify) is not that one of fearful contempt so popular among "critics" of radical and conservative persuasion, nor that one of unctuous submissiveness so popular among television and radio executive and advertising men. If they have an optimism, however muted, it is because they hold that every gain is not a loss; that if the losses outnumber the gains, nonetheless they do not obliterate them. And that is the best we can do—learn to tell the gains from the losses, so [as] to hold on to them.

Third Programs (even on nonprime time!) are all very well. But the Home Service is for us too. [The Third Programme is the most highly intellectual of the BBC's three programing Schedules; the Home Programme is the next level.—Ed.] I think that the mass-communications authorities among us make a slight error in emphasis when they concentrate almost exclusively on promoting the cause of "serious" TV. The Lively Arts—the popular arts at their possible best—are increasingly neglected by such students, who are then forced into being too grateful for what the media men give us. The net effect is to indicate that they, therefore we, are "above" the popular (the mass) arts. It is the humanist's task to tell his mass-communications colleague that one can't get "above" his ambiance. But, of course, first the humanist must grant that the mass-communications man is not merely a lapsed humanist; and the mass-communications man must grant that the humanist is not just a frustrated elitist. I think that if they begin to talk with one another, they will learn that they both speak imperfect dialects of the same language.

Beyond this, there is social action—the general nature and direction of which I think is obvious enough from many of the second-, third-, and fourth-step studies I alluded to in the beginning. The danger is that we will try to take action without knowing why and on whose behalf. On *our* behalf—that's who; and that's why. We are all of us inevitably part-time members of the mass audience. We know enough to divide it, and ourselves as part of it, into the mass audience *per se* and the popular audience. And we know enough to promulgate the popular tastes to which we can allow ourselves to be committed.

So far we are losing the battle, because so far, we have, in our panic, not been quite able to conceive what it would be like to win it. Were we to be possessed of a truly popular culture as well as a truly elite culture, the condition of our lives would be such as to force us frankly to admit that popular culture played a significant part in our lives—as, in point of fact, it already does. In the unattainable utopia for which we must work (because if we are honest with ourselves, there is nothing else to do), the terms *popular* and *elite* would refer to books and music and pictures which differed in value not as regards the segment of the population which comprehended them but as regards the degree of comprehension which they demanded: *full* and *middle* culture we might call them; and have to add a third term, *minimal* culture. All segments of the population would have free access to all levels. In the nature of things, there would be more devotees to the last two than to the first; nonetheless it is most likely that a man devoted to full culture would give himself to middle and minimal culture too, and so strengthen them and the viable relationship, without foreclosure, which should exist among them. And it would happen, I suppose, that just because a man was capable of comprehending full culture, he would comprise part of an elite dedicated to serving his culture as a whole. From the *power* elite to the *cultural* elite; from *full power* as a mode of governance to *full culture*. For full culture would entail full responsibility, the fullest sense of humanity and community.

But, saying all this, the humanist is properly wary of his own speculations—lest they blind him to the facts of life. Yet he *must* speculate, in order that he may the more sharply look about him and see and assess and work to amend such facts. For he can't but know that the problem of popular as against mass culture is embedded in our task of salvaging our world. Which is to say, of salvaging ourselves. Mass culture most often is not only subculture but anticulture. It destroys culture, our means of working out a relationship between what we are and what we ought to be, and so would destroy us, and deliver us packaged— to whom? That is the true horror. For the lords of the media and their minions are not satanic or dictatorial or consummately villainous. Indeed, they would destroy themselves along with us —and all without really knowing what they are doing. In our brave new world we have reached the stage where we can destroy and package ourselves to no purpose whatsoever. For there would be neither sender nor receiver: just that glittering package. Mass culture truly bores from within, bores us to death, bores us in the name of entertaining us, bores us into the state where we don't know that we are being bored, where boredom becomes normalcy. Meanwhile, The Package awaits.

REFLECTIONS ON MASS CULTURE [8]

By and large, people seriously concerned with mass culture fall into three groups. There is first a nucleus of artists and literary men, supported by a few theoreticians. They feel isolated, alienated, submerged and pushed aside by mass culture; their hopes are dim and they detest it. The literati and the theoreticians are opposed by another group—the practical men, who have decided it is their duty to work for the mass media in spite of the opulent salaries pressed on them. Sedulously aided by academic fellow travelers, they resolutely defend popular culture and their own *sacrificium intellectus* [intellectual sacrifice].

The third and largest group stays squarely in the middle, although for motley reasons. Most sociologists are located here; they have been taught that to be anywhere else, particularly when cultural matters are involved, is unscientific. Besides, many of them lack the trained sensibility that would discriminate between, say, English prose and their own writing. Liberal philosophers, on the other hand, have investigated the impossibilities of justify-

[8] From article by Ernest van den Haag, adjunct professor of social philosophy, New York University, and member of the faculty of the New School for Social Research. *The American Scholar.* 29, no 2:227-34. Spring '60. Copyright © 1960 by the United Chapters of Phi Beta Kappa. By permission of the publishers.

ing value judgments for so long that they regard anyone criticizing mass culture for moral or aesthetic reasons as bold but naïve. There is no evidence, they seem to say, for practically any view; hence, let's close our eyes and discuss methodology.

With all that, liberal philosophers seem to stress, somewhat unilaterally, the lack of evidence for negative views of mass culture. Perhaps they feel uneasy with rejections of mass culture because of political fears—misplaced ones, in my opinion. They seem unable to free themselves from the suspicion that a rejection of mass culture implies a rejection of the masses (although the contrary is no less logical) and is, therefore, antidemocratic. However, this is a *non sequitur*. One might think little of the cultural capacity of the masses but not therefore of their political capacity. But even if one thinks little of their political competence, one might still feel that there is no reason why they should not suffer, benefit and possibly learn from its use (and no more is needed to argue for democracy). Finally, although one might be somewhat pessimistic about the masses, one might be even more so about the political capacity of restricted groups. At any rate, neither mass culture nor objections to it seem to promote specific political views: Fascists and Communists, as often as liberals, favor mass culture, although they occasionally borrow some phrases from its opponents.

Historians, who of all men might be expected to discern the uniqueness of mass culture, seldom do. When they pay heed to mass culture as a historical phenomenon, they seem to take the wrong cue. Thus, Stuart Hughes recently observed, in a perceptive paper, that "our students yawn over the classics" because they have "very little to do with their own lives." He implies that we might as well forget about the classics. This seems odd. Students have always yawned over the classics—only, in times past, teachers were not so sensitive to their own popularity rating nor so eager to entertain their students as to be willing to drop the classics. They dropped some yawning students instead and kept the interested ones. An immature mind cannot understand the classics; and it matures, in part, by learning to understand them—or, at least, to know them so that they may be understood later. Students brought up in an age of rapid technological change may be convinced that literature, like machinery, is subject to obsolescence—a conviction some teachers share or dare not oppose enough to crack the shell. Perhaps this is what makes the classics seem irrelevant.

Yet the classics, if truly classic, cannot be irrelevant, for they deal with subjects relevant to the universal human predicament in ways to be re-experienced perennially. Of course, it is possible that we have become irrelevant to the classics: if our lives have lost all meaning, then no literature worthy of that name can be meaningful to us. For it is the possible meaning of human life that classic literature explores; and we cannot be interested without any experience of meaning and style in our own lives. If we have no such experience, then entertainment bereft of meaning—diversion from boredom, time killing, mass culture—is all that remains. In this case, the relevant must become ir-relevant, and only what is irrelevant to begin with can be absorbed. But I'm not yet willing to give up altogether. Under favorable conditions, the study of literature helps us see the possibilities of man's career on earth.

While some are ready to yield to those bored by high culture, others are convinced that the mass media can serve, indeed do serve, to bring high culture to the masses, and that in doing so they justify their existence or, at least, render an important service. Popular magazines may have authors such as Norman Vincent Peale, the argument goes, but don't they also publish an occasional uncensored article by Bertrand Russell? They do. However, a piece by a major philosopher does not make a philo-sophical magazine out of *Look*—it may make a popular journalist out of the philosopher. In the stream of, at best, diverting banalities, the worth-while piece tends to disappear without impact. It may seduce a Russell to lower his standards and write more such pieces, becoming less worth while and more acceptable in the process. It won't lure *Look* readers into the *Principia Mathematica*. Mass culture can be decorated with high culture pieces without being otherwise changed.

Note further that Russell's opinions are not offered to *Look* readers because of their intrinsic merit; they are offered because they are *his* opinions. Russell is by now a public figure, which means that he can be published without being taken seriously. Had I written the same words, I could not have broken into *Look*, precisely because people might have taken the utterance seriously instead of gobbling it up with the rest of the fare, while captivated by the utterer's fame.

Not everybody defends the mass media as vehicles that bring elements of high culture to the masses. Some depict the culture of the masses, articulated by the mass media in their normal offerings, as superior to high culture to begin with. Thus, one of mass culture's most faithful admirers, Mr. Gilbert Seldes, recently explained that he thinks more highly of Charlie Chaplin than of Marcel Proust because the former has brought more happiness to more people than the latter. Now happiness is hard to measure, and I am not sure that it makes sense to compare the feeling of a person reading Proust to that of another seeing Chaplin. We may grant, however, that more persons have been amused and diverted by Chaplin than by Proust. Still more people are made happy or are diverted by whiskey, apple pie, penicillin, Marilyn Monroe or, perhaps, by a movie that Mr. Seldes and I might agree is thoroughly bad. In short, making people happy is a criterion only if that is what one sets out to do—and I doubt that this was Proust's purpose or the purpose of any serious writer. Surely more persons enjoy Rodgers and Hammerstein than Bach—more enjoy Liberace than Glen Gould. By definition, popular culture is enjoyed by more people than high culture. Mr. Seldes' view would sanction the elimination of art in favor of entertainment—high-class entertainment, at best.

And this is precisely what I am afraid of. Mass culture demands entertainment and so extravagantly rewards those who provide it with money, prestige and power that serious artists become isolated—and tempted. To be sure, such tendencies have always existed; but now they prevail. The strength of the offerings of mass culture, compared with those of art, has risen immensely, and the dividing line has been blurred.

The chances for the values of mass culture to be internalized in childhood also have greatly increased, so that what I have described as temptation is not felt to be such, but on the contrary, as the due reward for well-directed, talented efforts. The view held by Mr. Seldes in all innocence is widely accepted by less articulate persons. It is a very basic American view, a naïvely pragmatic and philanthropic view that refuses to recognize what cannot be tangibly measured in terms at once hedonistic and altruistic. The measurement for art thus becomes the number of people made happy—and as soon as this becomes the end of art, art ends.

The answer to those who oppose pessimistic views on mass culture lies here. They argue that there is no evidence that the masses are culturally worse off. (I suspect they are far from well off, but comparisons are nearly impossible.) As far as the elite is concerned, they ask what prevents it from being as creative as ever? Why can't it coexist with mass culture? Haven't there always been several coexisting levels of culture? Can't we have a pluralistic society?

This reasonable argument overlooks the historically most distinctive and important characteristic of mass culture: the dominant power of the mass of consumers over production, public opinion and prestige. The elite in the past was sufficiently isolated and protected from the masses (which, properly speaking, did not exist as such) to be able to cultivate its own garden. And the mass market (hardly in existence) had nothing much to offer. Further, power, income and prestige distribution being what they were, the masses had no desire to impinge on the culture of the elite; on the contrary, they made room for it. At any rate, if they had a wish to participate or encroach, they had no way of making their demands felt and of articulating them. (Even political revolutions, before Hitler, were led and inspired by members of the elite.) But this has changed. We all now cultivate cash crops in market gardens. Mass culture is manufactured according to the demands of the mass market. No *independent* elite culture is left, for mass culture is far too pervasive to permit it. Cultivated individuals and islands of high culture remain, of course. But they are interstitial and on the defensive even when admired and respected; indeed, then more than ever, for they easily may be "taken up" and typecast. The intellect when alive is not part of our social structure, nor does it have its own domicile.

A convinced egalitarian may ask, So what? No more elite, no more high culture; but the great majority of people—who never belonged—have what they wish. To be sure, most people never were, are not now, and are unlikely ever to be interested in high culture. Yet, it does not follow that high culture is unimportant. Its importance cannot be measured by the number of people to whom it is important. Political issues may be decided by majority vote (or, at least, by letting the majority choose who is to decide them). This is surely not a good way, but nevertheless, I think, the best available.

However, the analogy between political issues and cultural issues (or, for that matter, moral ones) is inappropriate. Political issues, by whatever means they are decided, require collective action. Taxes cannot be levied only on those who feel they benefit proportionately from a pattern of public expenditure, or on individuals who are willing to vote for them. With art and literature it is otherwise, or it was. They could be cultivated by intellectual elites, without mass participation. This is becoming less possible every day. Mass culture threatens to decide cultural issues by a sort of universal suffrage. This is a threat to culture, not an occasion for rejoicing. For once cultural issues are regarded as indivisible, the majority view will prevail—and the majority prefers entertainment to art. Yet, unlike properly political matters, cultural ones do not require collective action, but rather that the mass of people and the law do not interfere. Culture cannot be created by political actions, although it can be destroyed by them. (The support of social groups is required, of course, but not that of society—or of masses—except inasmuch as it makes the existence of the social groups possible.) There would never have been any serious art, philosophy or literature if a majority vote had decided whether a given work was to be created and presented.

Yet, even if these things are important only to a few people, they are the best and most important people, the saving remnant. Actually, these things and these people are important even to those who ignorantly sneer at them. Such feelings as love; such experiences as wit, beauty or moral obligation; or styles of congress, housing and living—all, however degenerate they may become, are brought into existence and elaborated by artists and intellectuals. Without them, life is formless. With them, there is, at least, a paradigm. The most common of human experiences and the most trite still depend on artists and intellectuals to become fully conscious and articulate. Even the silliest entertainer and his public are part of, or are parasites of, a long line of creators of cultural expression—artists, philosophers, writers, composers, et cetera. For as Bernard Berenson suggested, "Popular art is always a derivation from professional individual art." Just as the technician depends on pure scientists he may never have heard of, so civilized nations in general depend on the creators of cultural expression—intellectuals and artists. The relation of the cultural elite to the masses may be compared to the relation of the saints and the cloistered to the faithful at large. Or, the cultural elite may be compared to the playwrights and the actors on stage, whose words, actions, costumes and settings are of significance to the spectators across the footlights, even though they are but spectators.

Although few people become outstanding mathematicians, scholars and artists, or understand what these are doing, society must permit those who cultivate such activities their separate existence or cease to be civilized. And the loss and degeneration of civilization injures everyone—the living and the unborn generations for whom we should hold in trust their rightful heritage. It is not enough, either, to permit some individual specialists to go their way. We need an intellectual and artistic elite (joined, of course, by merit) supported by a necessarily restricted and therefore discriminating public, both with reasonably continuous traditions. If this elite is not allowed autonomy and self-cultivation, if instead it is induced to follow mass tastes and to cater to them, there can be no cultural creation. We may parasitically ring a few changes on the culture of the past; we may find ways to entertain ourselves; but we won't have a style and an experience of our own.

I should not object to cultural pluralism—to mass culture co-existing with high culture—if it were possible. (Folk culture is long dead—although many people don't know a zombie when they see one.) A universally shared high culture is, of course, absurd and self-contradictory. This may sound snobbish, but I didn't make the world; I'm merely describing it. Talents as well as intelligence and sensitivity to various values are differentially distributed. We are lucky if 1 or 2 per cent of the population can be creative in any sense and 15 to 20 per cent can cultivate some sensibility. The remainder benefits indirectly.

The trouble with mass culture is that in various direct and indirect ways it tends to make the existence of high culture impossible. In our eagerness to open opportunity to everybody, we have greatly diminished the prizes available to anybody. Good wine is hard to cultivate when it is habitually diluted and we are brought up to be indiscriminate. We might do well to abandon the sterile and injurious attempts to "improve" mass culture, for its main effect is to debase high culture by "bringing it to the masses." What we must do is to bring some gifted people—not masses—to high culture. We must concentrate on finding ways to save and transmit high culture independently of the culture of mass society. My own view is pessimistic. I should like nothing better than to be proved wrong.

THE CULTURE MACHINE [9]

Who can forget the remorseless feeding machine in Charlie Chaplin's *Modern Times?* The machine is intended to eliminate the lunch hour in the factory in which Chaplin works. It goes berserk. Spoons jab into Chaplin's mouth, a corn cob grinds relentlessly against his teeth, soup spatters over his shirt, a napkin punctuates the meal with ferocious mechanical stabs. The only nourishment Chaplin gets is a pair of steel nuts that another worker inadvertently plunks on a plate.

The feeding machine comes irresistibly to mind when one contemplates the culture boom in the United States. It is as if one were strapped into a Kulturvac 112B that spews forth classical records, paperbacks, poetry readings, Shakespeare festivals, little theatres and big cultural centers. The machine is out of control, and at every turn one is pummeled by the artifacts of culture. It is unsafe to buy a toothbrush at a drug store—Kierkegaard, the Dead Sea Scrolls, Henry Miller, the Bhagavad-Gita and Jane Austen are all a brooding presence on the paperback rack, silently frowning at a mere commercial transaction.

The other week in New York I talked with an executive of the Crowell-Collier Company, a firm that used to publish a slick weekly magazine and that still turns out encyclopedia sets of costly girth. Crowell-Collier has turned to paperback books, and in the first year six hundred titles whirled from the presses— everything from six volumes of Santayana and three different biographies of Cromwell to the secrets of Jewish cookery. My informant explained that C-C was sick of the "smoking jacket and curved-pipe approach to literature." He was full of no-

[9] From article by Karl E. Meyer, American author and journalist. *New Statesman.* 65:38. Ja. 11, '63. Reprinted by permission.

nonsense facts and figures. At C-C, I was firmly told, every product from Agatha Christie to Zen Buddhism was judged in terms of "stock turnover and dollars per square foot."

The total inventory of all paperback publishers now consists of some twelve thousand titles. *Publishers' Weekly* noted last week that about 44 per cent of the annual estimated sales of $133 million is at drug stores, erstwhile symbol of soulless materialism. Sales records convey a surrealistic picture of the American mind—Mickey Spillane is right up there with Dr Spock; but then *To Kill a Mockingbird,* a sensitively written novel, . . . was a runaway best-seller last year. J. Edgar Hoover does well, and so did the late C. Wright Mills, whose *Listen, Yankee!,* a pro-Castro tract, sold about half a million copies. Distributors of paperbacks offer their wares with the disinterested zeal of a supermarket vending rival brands of frozen succotash. . . .

In the past two years, Kulturvac 112B has been anointed by White House patronage. . . . To raise money for a National Cultural Center in Washington . . . in sixty cities, a total of 150,000 persons squeezed into ninety theatres and hotel ballrooms to see a closed-circuit Pageant of the Arts, while another 200,000 paid to watch the show on pay-TV at home.

The main event in Washington was a $100-a-plate dinner staged in the huge Armory where you could stare at the President and his Cabinet over platefuls of steak and peppermint ice cream. The Pageant itself was an earnest vaudeville of the arts. The program included Danny Kaye, Pablo Casals, a long half hour of a *Long Day's Journey,* Yo-Yo Ma (a nine-year-old musical prodigy) and the inescapable Leonard Bernstein, master of ceremonies, who explained Why Culture Is Important. Not a detail was missed by Kulturvac 112B—free mentholated cigarettes, miniature whiskey bottles nesting in plastic bags, and gold-embossed match boxes advertising Hertz Rent-a-Car adorned each table in the Armory, like the steel nuts plunked on Chaplin's machine.

The next round of the cultural center campaign takes place later this year. It will be even bigger and better—a fine arts auction, "the largest of its kind in history." A half dozen cities are expected to participate; bids will be submitted through closed-circuit television for everything "from a Rembrandt to a Picasso, from an Aubusson tapestry to a Ming vase." Star-studded? Of course. The "social and cultural occasion of the year?" Certainly: a case of *Life* imitating art.

Yet inevitably Kulturvac 112B rouses Luddite impulses. No one has thwacked it more than Dwight Macdonald, whose new collection of essays, *Against the American Grain,* contains a systematic attack on every premise behind mass-produced culture. The thesis is summed up neatly on the jacket blurb: "In trying to level down the best, Mr. Macdonald argues, our democratic society has usually succeeded in leveling up the worst, so that high and low culture merge in a swampy middle ground where second-rate writers are acclaimed as geniuses, first-rate writers retreat into private worlds, and the language itself begins to decompose."

Macdonald is for two cultures—one for the masses, one for the elite: any attempt at democratic compromise results in Midcult, the squashy and tepid stuff produced by Thornton Wilder, James Gould Cozzens and Archibald MacLeish. American magazines are insipid and fact-obsessed; American intellectuals betray their calling by lending comfort to such vulgarizations as the Great Books, the Revised Standard Version of the Bible and the third edition of Webster's *Unabridged* (which abdicates the prescriptive duties of a dictionary). And so forth.

The interesting contrast is with H. L. Mencken, a writer whose niche Macdonald has in some ways come close to filling. Both find democracy wanting and look with envy on societies with aristocratic features (Macdonald likes England; Mencken longed for the Germany of Bismarck). Both use the language like a Gatling gun, and both are remarkable for the vigor and variety of their indignation. The major difference is in targets. Mencken's lethal shafts were directed at the lowbrows—the fundamentalists, the boosters and boobs—and at those highbrows like Paul Elmer More who typified an arid genteel tradition. Mencken's attack was so withering that he altered the cultural landscape; more than anyone else, he helped make American democracy safe for James Joyce and D. H. Lawrence.

Times change, and the enemy for Macdonald has become the middlebrow, the fellow who knows all about art but who isn't sure what he likes. The reader of *Harper's,* the member of the Book-of-the-Month Club, the art theatre customer—this is the fellow that Macdonald stomps and bites and abuses. Yet how does the victim react? He yips with delight. In his day, Mencken got so much abuse from the pulpit and press that he blithely published a volume of selections, *Menckeniana: A Schimp-flexikon.* But Macdonald is praised by the Midcult organs and is attacked mainly in small and obscure journals. Last week, *Time,* the magazine he taunts the most, gave its beamish blessings: "One of the truly free-wheeling minds of the times." (Said the cheerful caption under his picture, "Against the ooze and ahs of Midcult.")

Surely this is the most insidious feature of Kulturvac 112B. It is programed to cope with every type of attack. Call it the vilest names, accuse it of every cultural crime, and bzzzzzt! a transistorized feed-back punches a tape and makes the attack itself part of the machine. You can't lick it. It joins you. When that all-star auction for the National Cultural Center takes place, I wouldn't be surprised if a cellophane-wrapped manuscript of *Against the American Grain* were offered up for sale. With Leonard Bernstein collecting the bids.

III. GOVERNMENT SUPPORT
FOR THE ARTS

EDITOR'S INTRODUCTION

While the arts may be a necessity to civilization, they remain an economic luxury. They are not, and they have never been, self-supporting. Someone or some institution must pay for them. In the Middle Ages in Western Europe the Church was the great patron of the arts. In the Renaissance patronage moved into individual hands—monarchs like Francis I, members of families like the Medici—where it remained substantially until contemporary times. Postwar inflation and the increasing economic complexity of modern society have tended in recent years, however, to reduce the role of the individual art patron. In Europe the responsibility for support of the arts has been assumed almost totally by the state. The forms and types of support—and their consequences—range widely from absolute state patronage and control in the totalitarian states to modified subsidy in the democratic nations.

In America the individual patron has incorporated and consolidated himself into the foundation. The names of Rockefeller, Ford, Guggenheim, Eastman, et al. no longer stand only for individuals but for highly organized structures that dispense vast sums in fellowships and grants to individual artists, in endowments to schools, museums, and libraries. Until recent years these foundations have been strictly private. Government support of the arts in America has been limited to a kind of vague paternal interest—an occasional commissioning of an artist to paint a mural in a post office, design a Government building or medal or postage stamp. A rare venture into more active Government patronage like the WPA theatre and art projects of the 1930's was the result of the desperate economic emergency of that period. It produced much sound and significant work, especially in the field of experimental drama, and reached a public which would otherwise have had little or no access to culture in any form. But it also generated hot political controversy, by which it was ultimately destroyed.

The fear of political interference and Government control is a real and telling one in America. Nevertheless, rising costs and pressures have made it inevitable that some more active part must be taken by Government on both the local and the national levels if American culture is to flourish. In June 1963 John D. Rockefeller 3d, chairman of New York's Lincoln Center for the Performing Arts, said in a speech to the American Symphony Orchestra League that America's rapidly expanding cultural life could not be supported by private philanthropy alone; costs could not be covered without Government help.

So widespread is the recognition of a need for some Government support of the arts that in the national presidential campaign of 1960 both the Democratic and Republican candidates were asked to express their views on the subject. Both warned against the potential dangers of Federal subsidy, but they agreed on the need for establishing Government advisory councils on the arts. Upon his election the late President John F. Kennedy made it clear that his expressed interest in the arts was more than mere campaign oratory. The dramatic appearance at his inauguration of the poet Robert Frost, the published lists of invited guests at the White House, including some of the most distinguished writers, artists, and musicians of the nation, and subsequently the active participation of President and Mrs. Kennedy in numerous cultural activities all served to create a spirit of cultural enthusiasm that swept the country. Mrs. Kennedy appeared on a nation-wide televised tour of the White House in which she guided the viewer as she knowledgeably discussed its art treasures. Largely through the influence of the Kennedys the "Mona Lisa" was sent to this country on loan from the Louvre. A widely publicized benefit, at which the Kennedys made a personal appearance, was given on closed-circuit television to raise funds for the National Cultural Center. This project, occupying nine acres along the Potomac, had been authorized by Congress in 1958, but up till the time of the benefit, work on it had been moving very slowly. After President Kennedy's tragic assassination the Center was renamed the John F. Kennedy Center for the Performing Arts and Congress appropriated $15.5 million for the project, matching donations in the same amount from private sources.

The risks involved in Government support of the arts are widely recognized—the threat of Government control, political

bias, the stifling of individual and independent activity so vital
to the creative process. Supreme Court Justice Arthur J. Goldberg,
who was first Secretary of Labor in President Kennedy's Cabinet,
examines the arguments for and against Government subsidy in
the article " 'To Come to the Aid of the Arts,' " reprinted in this
section. He concludes that since art is essential to a free society,
it must be supported by that society and that the best protection
against Government "interference" is vigilance against it. The
foundations for a positive program of action by the national
Government were laid with President Kennedy's appointment in
March 1962 of August Heckscher, director of the Twentieth Century Fund, to the newly created post of Coordinator of Culture.
Mr. Heckscher's job was to act as a liaison on cultural affairs
between the White House and Government and private agencies
and to survey "the relationship between the Government and
the arts in general." Although he had agreed to accept the
post for only six months, he remained until June 1963. Excerpts
from his report submitted upon resignation are included in this
section. From his long and careful study of all aspects of the
question Mr. Heckscher concluded: "Although Government's
role in the arts must always remain peripheral, with individual
creativity and private support being central, that is no reason why
the things which the Government can properly do in this field
should not be done confidently and expertly."

The trend seems clearly to be toward Government encouragement of the arts rather than outright patronage. That encouragement appears to be taking more concrete form in the sixties than
ever before. On the state and local levels, as Milton Esterow
reports in a New York *Times* article reprinted below, there has
been a widespread movement to create arts councils to stimulate
and encourage cultural pursuits. On the national level there is
the President's Advisory Council on the Arts, established in June
1963 following the release of Mr. Heckscher's report. This council will be composed of heads of Federal departments and agencies
concerned with the arts and thirty private citizens whose duty
it will be to survey the arts in the United States and "make
recommendations in regard to programs, both public and private,
which can encourage their development." The group was created
by presidential order because Congress continues to be reluctant
to act in such matters. But the steadily increasing interest in the

whole subject of Government support of the arts makes it likely
that the Advisory Council is a first step rather than a last one.
"Government can never take over the role of patronage and support filled by private individuals and groups in our society,"
President Kennedy wrote. "But Government surely has a significant role to play in helping establish the conditions under
which art can flourish—in encouraging the arts as it encourages
science and learning."

"TO COME TO THE AID OF THE ARTS" [1]

It has been said of Americans that we are respected for what
we can do but not for what we are, that we know how to work
but not how to live. Much of this is mere caviling by those who
are blind to the drive, the hard pragmatic realities and the absorbing challenge of American history, and who would judge a
people on the posture of their arts rather than their sum of
achievements in the economic and political and social fields.

At the same time, it is a useful reminder to us that the condition of the arts is a vital question in any society—and should
be so especially in ours, with its ideals of measurement of worth
by individual, not mass, standards. President Kennedy's . . .
appointment of August Heckscher, director of the Twentieth
Century Fund, as White House cultural coordinator is an indication that the arts will enjoy greater consideration in the environment of public policy than has been their fortune in the past.

How is it with the arts in America today? Their condition
can be described as extremely healthy in one aspect, but extremely hazardous in another.

There is a great difference between interest in the arts and
support for the arts. There is an even wider difference between
the cultural life we enjoy and what we might enjoy. The total
figures measuring artistic activity in America are impressive
enough to convince one that a new era may be at hand; yet they
are less impressive when one looks at them in terms of the people
involved.

The Department of Labor's recent edition of the *Occupational
Outlook Handbook* includes for the first time a section on the

[1] From article by Arthur J. Goldberg, Justice of the Supreme Court of the United
States and former Secretary of Labor. New York *Times Magazine.* p 26+. Mr. 11, '62.
© 1962 by The New York Times Company. Reprinted by permission.

performing arts—musicians, dancers, actors and singers. The employment outlook as reported, based upon the most careful and extensive surveys and interviews within each occupation, can only be described as bleak. Employment opportunities in each of the fields are limited and highly competitive. The earnings are not large, and in the case of many artists, employment is intermittent.

We do not have too many artists; we have too few opportunities for them. It is true that the artist will practice his art even under the most difficult conditions, but it is also true that, in a nation as prosperous and progressive as our own, there is no reason why the artist cannot be productive *and* reasonably compensated. In proposing my own six-point solution, I admit to some basic convictions.

First, I believe a flourishing cultural life is an essential, not an ornament, to the health and strength of a free society.

Second, I doubt if economic success is a proper or meaningful test of the value of the arts, and especially the fine arts. Whether they are able to support themselves at the box office is the least meaningful criterion of their true value.

Third, I believe it is well within the proper responsibility of Government in providing for the general welfare to do its part to help rescue troubled art forms from obsolescence.

In a complex, modern society like our own, art of all kinds is called to one of the essential services of freedom—to free man from the mass. Art—whether on a stage, in a gallery, or in a concert hall—asserts the supremacy of the individual. The insight of the artist leads to cultural discovery for all of the people. No one who has known the impact of a great artist's work can fail to appreciate the legend of Michelangelo who went in the dark of night to his studio, inflamed by the rumor that a competitor had laid claim to his statue "Pietà," and chiseled across the ribbon of the gown the inscription, still deep-etched to this day, "I, Michelangelo, made this."

My second conviction—that economic success is not a proper criterion for judging the value of either the artist or his art—is controversial to the extent that it goes against the grain of an affluent middle class with a tendency to measure the value of an art form in terms of financial worth or personal status. One dire result of this tendency is "made taste," whereby a publisher, an art dealer or a producer peddles price and sensationalism in place of quality. There is great contempt for the arts in attitudes that reduce them to investments, status symbols or vehicles for sensationalism.

The danger, of course, is that those art forms without commercial value lead a precarious existence on the edge of extinction. This works to the extreme disadvantage of the artist who may feel impelled to try to become financially successful merely to justify himself in terms of the society around him.

In the same way, artistic institutions are suspect if they are not able to stand the test of competition—as though opera and professional football were similar profit-making ventures and a loss at the box office a fit prelude to failure for both.

To free our art forms from destructive financial tests is to protect them from the tyranny of the majority. Alexis de Tocqueville, whose observations on democracy are illuminating to generation after generation, feared that democracy might fail precisely because the majority will would lead to the triumph of conformity and mediocrity. It has certainly been one of the great failures of the television industry that it has been subservient to the will of the majority, as measured by "experts," and in reaching for the most common of artistic denominators has rejected the aspirations of the minority, even though that minority may number several millions of people.

In sum, if art is essential to a free society, then it must be supported and encouraged and helped to flourish. If the arts are to flourish, they must be relieved of total dependence upon the market place, and upon majority opinion and taste.

I recommend a six-point partnership for the support of the arts in America. It is predicated on acceptance of the arts as a new community responsibility and is based on the principle of diversity and variety. The members of the partnership are the public, private patrons and benefactors, corporations, labor organizations, local and state governments, and the Federal Government. Each of the partners has a distinct responsibility.

Regardless of any subsidy the principal source of financial support for the arts must continue to be the public. An art form without an audience ceases to have meaning. And how many times have we heard people decrying the state of an art form like the theatre but seldom attending and offering no support?

There are aesthetic problems in public support, of course. If the theatre or the ballet do not offer living art to the public, then the public might well turn away. It is the responsibility of the artist to merit public support. A viable art requires a voluble public. Whatever its form—whether through increased participation in season subscriptions or through special contributory associations—public support is the keystone to artistic vitality, and the public must expect to provide a greater portion of the costs.

This is not to discount the continually vital role played by the second group of partners—those individual patrons and benefactors who have been bearing the main burdens for support of institutions like the Metropolitan Opera, and through whose generosity many communities now enjoy great art museums and other cultural resources. Furthermore, in a period of artistic experimentation such as our own, many of the best artists will run ahead of, or even contrary to, the general standards of the time. They will be forging ahead, leaving general public attitudes and perceptions far in their wake. Here the support of enlightened patrons can have the most profound and fruitful consequences.

Thirdly, the American corporation, a center of unprecedented power and wealth, has only recently awakened to the value of the arts as a complement to architecture and as a medium by which the "image" of the business can acquire distinction. While many corporate executives are sponsors of the arts, and some companies help support the arts in their communities, the corporation as an entity has not, as a rule, considered support for the arts in the same light it has support for educational, charitable and health activities. One can hardly walk into a corporate building erected in the past five years without noticing the painting and sculpture that adorn the reception rooms and private offices—work often done on commission. But thus far, the contributions of business to the arts remain only a fraction of its generous contributions to other community needs.

This is true, also, of the funds and foundations that have risen from corporate fortunes. It may be impossible even to suggest an adequate proportion of expenditure for the arts; a review of the statements of our largest funds and foundations, however, reveals what appears to be comparative neglect of such support. When two noted American funds recently offered assistance to a Washington repertory theatre, Arena Stage, for example, it was the first such artistic venture for one.

Even more important, in my view, would be the great vote of confidence in the American artist that corporations could cast through their advertising. Each year, truly vast sums of money are poured into corporate advertising—yet the amount that involves the fine arts is relatively small, and the art forms sponsored by advertisers are few.

A responsibility similar to that of corporations is the one that attaches to the American labor movement, which by its nature is pledged to the betterment of the American community. Labor unions have been slow, on the whole, to develop specific forms of support for the arts—but the exceptions, like sponsored concerts for children and the showing of paintings in union-sponsored exhibitions—are notable. They indicate what can be done, and should be done in larger measure.

The next large partner in the program of diverse support is the local government—the primary source of public support for the arts. A subsidy program that resulted only in large collections of art works in big cities, showing only to certain urban audiences, would defeat its own purpose. Art grows out of the life and spirit of a community; the artist reaches for his inspiration to the world around him, and today art, more than any other enterprise, preserves the intimate and personal nature of American life outside mass institutions.

Today, communities willingly provide housing and custodial care for art collections and historical museums; one wonders why more of them should not provide for operas, ballets, symphonies and local repertory theatres as well. Universities now make provision for professors-in-residence and artists-in-residence; why shouldn't municipalities?

The sixth partner is the Federal Government. I believe one of the most important immediate steps which the Federal Government should take is to establish a Federal Advisory Council on the Arts.

At present, the interest of the arts in America is represented in the councils of the Federal Government only in the individual attitudes of members of government, encouraged by the example of President and Mrs. Kennedy.

But still the artist is without the kind of representation that will permanently insure that his interests are heard regardless of prevailing attitudes.

A Federal Advisory Council, composed largely of artists themselves, would provide that representation. The field of the arts is, at present, rich in one aspect—in ideas and proposals to improve the economic status of the individual artist, and to rescue endangered art forms from economic oblivion. But there are few formal vehicles by which these ideas can be examined and brought to reality. There is, especially, almost a total lack of public policy in regard to the arts, at a time when many proposals —such as those relating to taxation—bear directly upon public policy. The council would have those two most important assets —undistracted concentration on its subject, and a voice of prestige and formal influence.

As a national clearinghouse of ideas, the council could have an effect not only upon the making of public policy in regard to the arts but also in influencing national attitudes regarding them. Its proposals would be designed as much to encourage private initiative as to influence governmental action. By keeping constantly alert to the status of our cultural resources, the council would also be alert to ways to maintain and increase them.

One much-needed function in the arts field is that of liaison. While there are many strong and independent spokesmen in each of the artistic disciplines, there is no agency that can approach or cooperate with local and state governments and private institutions on a permanent, statutory basis so that public policy is a coordinated whole serving the art community. Short of individual bills by congressmen and individual petitions to state and local governments, art is the orphan of American public policy.

What is to prevent the realization of this needed assistance? Those who flatly rule out any and all Federal participation in a support program for the arts generally hold one of two views, sometimes both: tax dollars should not be spent for what one writer called "a luxury in life"; and if tax dollars were to be spent, inevitable Government control of the arts would follow.

The first of these objections is based on a misunderstanding of my proposal, which does not envision large Federal outlays. But the second is voiced by those who are genuinely concerned about the freedom of artistic expression, and their concern is not to be dismissed lightly. Distinguished critics have reminded us of the shortsighted and often shabby treatment some artists have experienced at the hands of politicians. Others have marked the tendency of Government to watch its money carefully and attempt to set standards for its use.

I might say that this live sense of danger is in itself the best guarantee that we could have for artistic freedom. Also, the very concern that the arts might be subjected to control is additional evidence that they are relevant and important in American life and opinion.

Regardless of how the arts are supported, there will be efforts from some quarters to control their content. The question is— what measure of success do those efforts enjoy?

We should be perfectly honest and open about the problem of interference with the freedom of the arts and attempts to compromise the integrity of the artist. To close our eyes to the problem is neither right nor necessary—but what is necessary is to provide for safeguards against it. One of the reasons I have advocated a Federal Advisory Council on the Arts is the value of such a body in standing between the artist and the direct political process that might affect him.

We should acknowledge also that the market place exerts its own forms of censorship which can be as unyielding and rigid as any feared by opponents of subsidy. I received a letter from an artist in Texas who described to me his feelings at being asked to rush several paintings to a New York gallery for a showing, and then receiving them back with high praise but apologies that they were "too controversial." Every summer theatre and repertory theatre has had the experience of having to fall back on standard successes or suffer ruin. Subsidy, in short, may be less a straitjacket than the box office.

The object of my proposals is to free the artist, not bind him. The best protection against the danger of interference—admitting full well that the danger exists—is a community that recognizes it and is prepared to cope with it.

At the same time, there are certain policies that lessen the danger of interference, if they do not eliminate it. One of these is the principle that public support is most successful, and least subject to abuse, when it represents only a portion of the total funds involved. The matching grant should be the basic form of Federal participation in support of the arts with the Federal share always representing the smaller of the funds involved. One of the guiding ideas of the six-point partnership I propose is that artists are likely to retain maximum control over their work when a maximum number of governments, institutions and individuals are contributing to their support.

The final solution lies, of course, only with a larger and more active art public. Assistance of all kinds to the arts should include provisions whereby more people in more places have access to the arts, so that the dilemma of the artist will eventually find its best and happiest solution in an increased clientele and a sympathetic public. I do not propose state-supported institutions, such as exist in many European countries. A free democratic society can compete and succeed in a free, democratic way.

In discussing the issue of support, none should lose sight of the object of support—the artist himself. The achievement of the American artist has been very great. That achievement will grow larger with time. It is given to us now to do what we can to foster it.

THE ARTS AND THE NATIONAL GOVERNMENT [2]

Government in the United States has not in the past showed consistent concern for the state of the arts. There have been moments, particularly the formative period of the Republic, when statesmen possessed the clear realization that the forms of art reflected the inner ideals of the social order. The planning of cities and the construction of public buildings were expected to match the concepts of order and human dignity inherent in the country's laws and institutions. This awareness was dimmed during most of the period of westward expansion and industrial progress. But in the twentieth century American Presidents again began to sense a relationship between Government and the health

[2] From Report to the President, May 28, 1963, by August Heckscher, Special Consultant on the Arts. United States Senate. (Doc. no 28) 88th Congress, 1st session. Supt. of Docs. Washington 25, D.C. '63. p 2-28.

of the cultural life. Before Franklin Roosevelt inaugurated immensely fertile experiments in this field, Theodore Roosevelt had brought to the White House artists, scholars, and poets; William Howard Taft had established the Commission of Fine Arts.

Since the Second World War the role of Government in the arts has been repeatedly stressed. In 1958 Congress passed legislation establishing the National Cultural Center. A report on "Art and Government" requested of the Fine Arts Commission by President Harry S. Truman surveyed the field methodically and formed a starting point for much of the work done by the Special Consultant in recent months. Significantly, too, when President Eisenhower established a Commission on National Goals, the cultural life of the United States was one of the areas subjected to inquiry.

These two trends—mounting popular enthusiasm for the arts and a growing concern on the part of the Government—came together at the start of the present Administration. Attendance at the inaugural ceremonies of outstanding artists, writers, and scholars was understandably hailed as signaling a new partnership in the national life. Reconstitution of the White House as a dramatic symbol of America's cultural heritage, and the hospitality provided to outstanding representatives of the intellectual and artistic community, carried further the idea that Government and art have a basic relationship.

Against this background the first Special Consultant on the Arts was named. It was understood that he would be concerned with the progress of the arts primarily as they affect, not our international posture, but the well-being, the happiness, and the personal fulfillment of the citizens of our democracy. In this sense the appointment, modest in scope and tentative in form though it was, marked the beginning of a new phase in the history of art and Government. . . .

The Arts and the Executive Agencies

The Federal Government touches the arts at many points. By its programs and activities it can affect the cultural life of the country in important ways. If all is done well, much will have been accomplished, not only in making the Government a setter of standards but in giving support to creative talent. . . .

THE ACQUISITION OF ART

Government in the normal course of its operations acquires
by purchase or commission a considerable number of works of
art. In this way, Government is a patron of the arts. It creates
a market for the work of artists; it sets an example to others,
including public and private bodies, which may have an important effect on the general cultural climate. Memorials, statues, murals, fountains, historic and decorative paintings—as well
as works of art for public museums—are among the objects
which Government in some degree or other makes its own.

The role of Government as a patron of the arts in this sense
could well be increased. Its support of the artist could be exemplified more directly than heretofore; and the resulting acquisitions could more effectively serve to make its buildings, its open
spaces, its collections of art, representative of the values of a
great people. If the Federal Government is niggardly in this
regard, can we expect any better of our states and municipalities?
An important recommendation of this report, therefore, is that
the Federal Government make it an objective to increase substantially the number and worth of the works of art which it
acquires.

Art is now acquired in a variety of ways and through a variety
of agencies. Three areas offer particular possibilities.

Government Collections of Art. The Federal institutions
chiefly concerned with the acquisition of art do a splendid job
within their resources and their authority of preservation, display,
and research. But the National Gallery, the Smithsonian Institution, and the Library of Congress have virtually no funds,
except more or less accidental private bequests, for adding to
their collections. As a result, these collections cannot be truly
representative either of our artistic heritage or of contemporary
American art.

The Commission of Fine Arts in 1953 recommended funds for
the purchase annually of American art by the National Collection of Fine Arts. This could become the one Federal collection
of traditional and contemporary American art and urgently requires attention and review, not only in regard to funds but
staff and space.

Public Buildings. A current list . . . of works of art commissioned in the last three years in connection with public buildings suggests that the harvest has been meager, though the General Services Administration is now attempting to practice a policy of using for fine arts one half of 1 per cent of the cost of buildings over $250,000. It is well known that whenever building budgets must be cut, art is the first amenity to go. A bill before the Congress has specified that up to 1 per cent of the cost of Federal buildings in the national capital area be set aside for the commissioning of fine arts decoration. This would be a highly desirable step, and the principle should be extended to Federal buildings throughout the country and abroad. Such a policy was in effect as a depression measure during the prewar Roosevelt Administration and has been recently adopted by some of our cities, notably Philadelphia. It is certainly to be hoped that in planning the new Pennsylvania Avenue, for example, sculpture will have a prominent place.

American Embassies. American embassies are important cultural outposts. The purchase by the Government of American art, supplemented by private gifts, could lead to a collection administered by the National Gallery or some other bureau of the Smithsonian Institution and displayed, perhaps on a revolving basis, in U.S. embassies. These works should not be considered "interior decoration," but as art representing the finest of American creative expression. (They should be supplemented by special exhibitions, stressing contemporary works, loaned for short periods through such private patrons as the International Council of the Museum of Modern Art and the Woodward Foundation.)

In addition, in a number of often unrecognized ways the Government is constantly "acquiring" art—by purchase, commission, or creation by its own designers and producers. Examples of such activities are the commissioning of official portraits, the photographic and film projects of a number of Federal agencies (for example, Department of Agriculture, USIA [United States Information Agency], and the departments of the armed services), and the continuing art projects of the Air Force and the Navy. (It is interesting in this connection that during the Cuban crisis the Navy sent an artist to Guantanamo, and an artist also was commissioned by NASA [National Aeronautics and Space Administration] to document the landing of astronaut Major Cooper.)

Too often, unfortunately, the criteria observed are solely documentary or functional. There is every reason why the Government should also provide for high standards of artistic excellence. The distinguished quality of the Farm Security Administration photographic programs during the depression years is widely recognized as an artistic achievement of which the nation is proud. In the selection of artists for public portraits or historic events we should as a matter of course wish to be represented by the best American talent, as we do in all other fields of endeavor, whether it be weapons, scientific developments, or public buildings. Clear recognition of this principle is hardly less important than the provision of adequate funds.

RAISING DESIGN STANDARDS

Many of Government's activities are related to the arts indirectly in that they consist of a normal part of its operations which may be done with a sense of beauty and fitness, or may be done tastelessly. Government is a printer and coiner; it strikes medals and makes stamps. It is also a building on a grand scale. Should it not consistently promote, as Pericles said in his funeral oration to the Athenians, a "beauty in our public buildings to cheer the heart and to delight the eye day by day"?

The task throughout this area is to inject into the process of planning and execution a concern for aesthetic standards, for the quality of good design and good workmanship. Different problems exist in a field so broad and varied, but across them all lie certain common approaches to excellence.

Government Posters—An Example. Government posters may be cited as an example of the way in which a seemingly utilitarian process—in this case the communication of simple facts or ideas—can be raised to the level of art. A group of Government posters collected for this survey by the Prints and Photographs Division of the Library of Congress shows how frequently inferior American work is to European in this field; it also reveals the difference of quality which exists between different initiating agencies. The USIA has issued some striking posters for its exhibitions abroad; the Department of Commerce, in encouraging foreign travel to the United States, has used photographs to good effect, combined with excellent typography. The Armed Forces recruiting and training services have done consistently good work. Elsewhere, too often, the Government communicates with its citizens on a banal and commonplace level.

Does it matter that the level of posters be raised to the level of the best now being produced by private enterprise and by governments abroad? It is a basic assumption of this report that it does matter. Everything done by the Government bears either the marks of excellence which we like to think characteristic of a free and great people, or else in some measure it betrays the Government and degrades the citizen. . . .

Public Buildings—A Major Area of Concern. The implementation of the President's directive of May 23, 1962, on "Guiding Principles for Federal Architecture" is of first importance.

This directive recommended a three-point architectural policy for the Federal Government. It restated in affirmative and contemporary terms the conviction held by Washington, Jefferson, and other early American statesmen that public buildings should set an example for public taste and in the words of the directive "provide visual testimony to the dignity, enterprise, vigor, and stability of the American Government." It recommended (1) the selection of distinguished designs that embody the finest contemporary American architectural thought, (2) the avoidance of an official style and the encouragement of professional creativity through competitions and other means, and (3) the special importance of landscaping and site development in relation to the surrounding area.

Positive steps should be taken to incorporate these principles in the policies and criteria governing *all* Federal programs concerned with construction and building. Periodic reports to measure how well we are doing in achieving these objectives might be required and could appropriately be the responsibility of the over-all panel suggested above.

A basic assumption of this report is that good design is not an added embellishment or an unnecessary extravagance. In fact, the position is taken that good design is economical. It strongly endorses that section of the directive on guiding principles which says:

The committee takes it to be a matter of general understanding that the economy and suitability of Federal office space derive directly from the architectural design. The belief that good design is optional, or in some way separate from the question of the provision of office space itself, does not bear scrutiny, and in fact invites the least efficient use of public money.

IMPACT ON THE CULTURAL ENVIRONMENT

We have been speaking of Government's responsibility in the design of specific objects, from postage stamps to buildings. But Government's responsibility does not stop there. Not always is it recognized how large a role Government plays in preserving cultural assets and creating an environment within which cultural values can be realized. Public buildings, if they are to be genuinely significant, must not only be well designed but must be part of a setting in which life can be lived with some sense of spaciousness, dignity, and aesthetic delight. Again, roads are not only per se susceptible of being improved in appearance and in the aesthetic experience they provide; what is even more important, they must be so conceived and carried out as not to dehumanize the landscape or run roughshod over the living community.

The scale upon which modern Government acts makes it vital that this responsibility to the total environment be acknowledged. The constant tendency is to think only of the immediate task, forgetting the wider implications of governmental action. The economics of roadbuilding too often threaten to run highways across historic towns, park lands, or even across a college campus. The urgency of slum clearance often means that a wrecking crew destroys in the process a humanly scaled and intricately woven community life. . . .

The Renaissance state has been referred to as "a work of art." Today the whole environment, the landscape and the cityscape, should be looked on as potentially a work of art—perhaps man's largest and most noble work. The power to destroy provided by modern organization and machinery is also, if it is wisely used, an unprecedented power to create. To create humanely in the service of man's highest needs is a supreme task of modern statesmanship.

PRESENTATION AND DISPLAY OF ART

Government responsibility is not discharged in acquiring and conserving works of art and other objects of historic and artistic merit. To be enjoyed and appreciated by the people and to make the contribution they should to our cultural life they must be made available and accessible in a much more extensive and varied manner than they have been to date. . . .

The National Collections. A positive program should be adopted to expand the educational and presentation activities of the national collections. The many excellent recommendations in this regard of the report to the President submitted by the Fine Arts Commission in 1953 should be carried out. In this report, the Commission urged that in addition to providing authority and funds to the national collection to make this a truly representative museum of American art, a greatly expanded program of traveling exhibitions, catalogs, and publications and reproductions should be initiated.

Much more attention should be given to the production of publications of distinction and high aesthetic standards.

Consideration should be given to organizing some central clearing system to coordinate such activities and to publicize their availability.

The much more extensive and imaginative use of public buildings, such as post offices and regional office buildings, for poster and exhibit displays, and even the distribution of Government publications, should be encouraged. A small pilot project to promote the sales of Government publications has just been instituted by the Post Office Department.

The basic objective is the use of the great resources of our national collections for the benefit and enjoyment of all the people throughout the country.

Presentation of the Performing Arts. The Federal Government should fulfill its responsibility for the performing as well as the visual arts. Government auditoriums have generally been built with little or no concern for this important function. The sponsorship of concerts and theatrical performances has been very limited, primarily restricted to the city of Washington, and in most instances entirely dependent on private gifts to the Government.

The programs of chamber music, literary readings, and dramatic performances taking place in the Library of Congress, the National Gallery Symphony Orchestra concerts, and the few programs, including experiments with "Son et Lumière," sponsored by the National Park Service, are the main examples. Tours and performances sponsored by the armed services provide an opportunity for presenting the performing arts to an audience which is in a position greatly to influence the future cultural life of American communities.

The National Cultural Center. Creation of the National Cultural Center will enhance the Federal Government's role in presenting American cultural achievements and in stimulating and supporting the performing arts throughout the country. To fulfill its aim, the Center must be more than a group of splendid stages for the benefit of Washington audiences.

The general policy of the Cultural Center is outside the scope of this report; but it may be stressed here that if it is to fulfill its role of presenting the performing arts to a broad national audience it must from the start conceive a program keyed to diverse and wide-ranging interests. Not only must it be expected to present the best of orchestras, repertory theatre, opera, choral and dance groups from this country and overseas; it must also reach out through competitions, festivals, youth programs, and commissioned works into the heart of the nation's cultural life. The motion picture, that most characteristic and indigenous of American art forms, should have an important place in the program. The organization of the motion picture industry tends to emphasize the expensive commercial feature picture. The Center can provide a means to encourage both the production and the opportunity for public viewing as well as a way of recognizing the best of our documentary and shorter fine arts films.

The Cultural Center must use all means to make its presentations extend beyond the area of its hall. A program of education and dissemination activities must be central in its planning.

Plans must be made for bringing the programs to the country at large through full use of television. . . .

Presentation in the International Sphere. Cultural exchange is one of the most important means by which Government fulfills its role of presenting and displaying American arts. The foreign policy aspects of this program are not considered here. It must be stressed, however, that the cultural life at home is stimulated and benefited by the effectiveness with which this responsibility is carried out. The recognition American artists receive through the exhibition of their works abroad is an important element in their development. Those who have the experience of working abroad and coming to know the artists of other countries bring back fresh skills and new sources of inspiration. (It is significant, for example, that the Jerome Robbins ballet, which played at the White House in 1962, was an American group tempered by three seasons at the Spoleto Festival.)

For these reasons it is urged that an active exchange program be furthered by all Government agencies directly or indirectly involved. Despite the proven value of these international programs and the great increase in the number of new countries we are trying to reach, there has been no increase in the relatively small amount of money allocated to the circulation of art exhibitions and the touring of performing arts groups. The average cost of a symphony orchestra tour runs to 25 per cent of the budget, and the tour of the American Repertory Theater, a company created to meet the demand for a professional American theatre tour, was so costly that its repetition cannot be reasonably contemplated within present budgets. Funds for traveling art exhibitions are totally inadequate. If these programs are to fulfill their purpose in demonstrating abroad the vitality and quality of the arts in the United States, adequate funds must be made available. . . .

GOVERNMENT RECOGNITION OF THE ARTIST

Most of the great countries of the world have traditionally given recognition not only to outstanding military and Government service but also to individuals for distinguished accomplishment in science, the arts, and the humanities. Britain has an Honors List; France the Legion of Honor and the Academy; the

Soviet Union a variety of awards. Japan gives recognition by designating her artists as "living cultural assets."

In recent years there has been growing support in the United States for a system of national recognition of achievement in the arts and the humanities. Presidential recognition has been given in several different ways through special dinners, individual invitations to the White House, and occasional performances by leading professional artists or youth groups. This method, however, is necessarily irregular and personal and can scarcely answer the requirements of a formal and continuing system, though a more official system does not, of course, exclude the continuation of the various forms of personal presidential recognition noted above, which have important values of their own.

A number of bills to establish a system of medals or awards in various fields of civilian endeavor have been introduced in Congress in recent years but have never been passed. An occasional individual, such as Robert Frost, has been honored by a medal authorized by special legislation. Until very recently, however, there has been no system of regularly honoring accomplishment or contribution in all fields of human endeavor. As a result of legislation passed in 1959, a National Medal of Science was established and the first award made in February 1963. Also in the scientific field are the Fermi and Lawrence Awards, which include cash prizes, and are granted by the Atomic Energy Commission, as authorized in its basic legislation, for meritorious contributions to the development of atomic energy.

The highest civil honor of the United States has been the Medal of Freedom originally established by President Truman as an award for meritorious service in connection with the war. Its scope and purpose has recently been broadened, and from now on it will be awarded on a systematic annual basis to a limited but unspecified number of persons who have made especially meritorious contributions to the security or national interests of the United States, world peace, cultural or other significant public or private endeavors.

There still seems a need, however, for an additional system of awards in specific art fields. The schemes adopted should be chosen carefully after thorough consideration of various alternative proposals, criteria and means of selection and consultation with the intellectual and artistic community. It is the recommendation of this report that the consideration of all proposals should be specifically assigned to the President's Advisory Council on the Arts.

The basic objective of a system of recognition should be to stimulate interest in and respect for intellectual and artistic effort and achievement.

Very careful thought should be given to the scope of the awards, the nature of the awards (should they include cash prizes or be purely honorary?), and the type of awards (should they recognize young talent, a specific achievement, accomplishments over a period of years, the winner of a specially held competition, or include several types and perhaps on a graduated scale of prestige?). The procedures, criteria, and membership of the selection system should be weighed especially carefully. The question of whether recognition should be restricted to American citizens or in some instances extended to foreigners should be discussed. . . .

General Policies Affecting the Arts

There is a broad range of general Government policies which are designed to accomplish objectives not primarily or specifically related to the arts, but which do affect and concern the state of the arts and the position of the individual artist, often adversely and mainly through inadvertence. These are in such fields as taxation, copyright laws, postal rates, disposition of surplus Government property, public works, and general assistance programs.

Of these, the impact of the tax laws is undoubtedly the most important, mainly because the earning and income pattern of the writer and artist differs strikingly from that of most other professions and occupations.

Our tax laws have traditionally been more concerned with providing relief and incentive to the "inventor" than to the "artist." The argument has been that tax relief to the inventor is necessary to encourage the inventive genius essential to economic growth. It is time that the contribution of the artist and writer to the cultural growth of society be given at least equal consideration. Nor need the artist be accorded special privileges. Revisions in tax laws and administrative interpretations which would recognize the distinctive character of his income pattern would of themselves go a long distance to remedy the artist's precarious economic plight. . . .

Administrative Machinery Relating to the Arts

Experience during recent months suggests the need for setting up continuing administrative means for dealing with issues of the arts. The public has come to anticipate that the expressed concern of the Government will be formalized in some way. It is important that nothing pretentious or heavyhanded be created, and equally important that recent initiatives not be allowed to expire. The following suggestions build upon what has already been done, and look ahead to what seems a natural development in the light of increased and deep-lying national interest in the arts.

These suggested steps presuppose a constant concern with the enhancing and development of the arts through normal activities of the Federal Government. They also look forward to a more direct involvement of government through a new institutional body with operating funds. They do not envisage any effort to direct or influence the work of artists; their purpose is to keep the arts free, not to organize or regiment them.

SPECIAL ADVISER

A major recommendation of this report is that the post of Special Consultant on the Arts be continued after the present trial period. Consideration should be given to its being full time and having the status of special adviser. Detailed day-by-day attention is necessary if governmental operations, often seemingly unrelated to the arts, are to be brought to the standards advocated by this report. . . .

Besides the policy planning and review functions which formed the major part of the original assignment, . . . [the special adviser] should be available for advice on all matters pertaining to the arts which arise in the course of the administration's work. He should be the President's liaison with the National Cultural Center, should sit in on panels and meetings where matters of Federal architecture, design, graphics, etc., are being discussed.

In addition, the special adviser should have, as described below, a close relationship with the President's Advisory Council on the Arts.

THE ADVISORY COUNCIL

Detailed recommendations relating to the establishment and functions of an Advisory Council within the Executive Office of the President have been separately submitted. This Council provides an essential part in an orderly and representative structure dealing with the arts. Its basic function is to continue and fill out the work of study and gathering information begun with the limited resources of the special consultant; to review Federal policies and make recommendations for improving design; to recommend long-range programs; and to assure the active participation of the artistic community in the Government effort.

The special adviser can call upon the Council and its specialized committees for assistance. The Advisory Council will thus become part of the machinery through which advice is provided to the various agencies of Government as they endeavor to set up art committees of their own, to organize competitions, or otherwise to raise the level of design.

The President will appoint the Chairman of the Council, who presumably will be the special adviser. Following experience in the science field, the Advisory Council should achieve effectiveness and stature through being related to the President's adviser and having its recommendations go through him directly to the President.

A NATIONAL ARTS FOUNDATION

An arts foundation, on the model of the existing foundations in science and health and as already proposed in legislation before the Congress, would appear to be the logical crowning step in a national cultural policy. Such a foundation would be a means of administering grants-in-aid, generally on a matching basis, to states and institutions of the arts. It might thus administer matching grants to states setting up arts councils. It might make available grants for demonstration projects proposed by particular cultural institutions. Thus it could consider helping support experiments designed to increase attendance, to foster creativity and introduce contemporary works to new audiences, or to offer services on an experimental basis. The foundation would not provide subsidies to carry the deficits of such institutions, but would aim at promoting cultural diversity, innovation and excellence.

Such an arts foundation should be thought of as supplementing the goals of the National Cultural Center, for it would help develop and stimulate the cultural activities and institutions of the country. And these, in turn, would have for their ultimate showcase the stages of the National Cultural Center in Washington.

What is sketched here represents the beginning of what could become a permanent policy giving form to the relationship between Government and the arts. It is a limited policy; for Government's role in this area must always be marginal. It is a policy not copied after European models, but keyed to the particular conditions of diversity and decentralization prevailing in the United States.

There will always remain those who feel that art and Government should exist in different spheres, having nothing to do with each other. But in fact the Government of the United States comes up constantly against choices and decisions where aesthetic considerations are involved. In today's world, moreover, artistic talent and creativity are resources vitally important to the nation, and the well-being of the people is related to progress in the arts as surely as to progress in fields such as recreation and education where Government's responsibility is fully recognized.

Although Government's role in the arts must always remain peripheral, with individual creativity and private support being central, that is no reason why the things which the Government can properly do in this field should not be done confidently and expertly.

THE PRESIDENT'S ADVISORY COUNCIL ON THE ARTS [3]

Establishment of an Advisory Council of the Arts has long seemed a natural step in fulfilling the Government's responsi-

[3] Statement by the late President John F. Kennedy establishing the President's Advisory Council on the Arts, June 12, 1963. In *The Arts and the National Government.* Report to the President, May 28, 1963, by August Heckscher. United States Senate. (Doc. no 28) 88th Congress, 1st session. Supt. of Docs. Washington 25, D.C. '63. p 33-4.

bility to the arts. I acknowledge the support of members of the Congress in both houses for this measure. I am hopeful that the Congress will give the Council a statutory base, but, meanwhile, the setting up of the Council by executive action seems timely and advisable.

Accordingly, I am establishing the President's Advisory Council on the Arts within the executive office, to be composed of heads of Federal departments and agencies concerned with the arts and thirty private citizens who have played a prominent part in the arts. Private members will be drawn from civic and cultural leaders and others who are engaged professionally in some phase of the arts such as practicing artists, museum directors, producers, managers, and union leaders. An executive order is being issued today defining the scope and structure of the Council, and I shall shortly announce the names of those private citizens I am asking to serve.

The creation of this Council means that for the first time the arts will have some formal Government body which will be specifically concerned with all aspects of the arts and to which the artist and the arts institutions can present their views and bring their problems.

It is my hope that the Advisory Council will keep the state of the arts in this country under survey, and will make recommendations in regard to programs both public and private which can encourage their development. I trust that the Council will recommend such permanent procedures and programs as they consider necessary in this field.

I should like to summarize briefly my reasons for believing that the establishment of such a Council by the Federal Government is both appropriate and urgent.

Widespread public interest in the arts has not always been accompanied by adequate concern for the basic institutions of our cultural life. Increased attendance at museums, for example, has not eased longstanding financial problems but has actually increased the strains on these institutions as new services have been expected by the public. Of the thousand and more symphony orchestras of which we are justly proud as a nation, only a comparatively few have serious professional status and offer a season of sufficient length to provide a living wage to performers. The same is even more true of opera and dance groups. For some years American singers have been going in large numbers to find in Europe opportunities for employment which institutions at home cannot provide. The professional theatre—despite the development of amateur groups—reaches only a limited part of the population. Indeed children are growing up who have never seen a professionally acted play.

A recent estimate by the Department of Labor presents a gloomy forecast on employment opportunities for the next decade. Although the demand for concerts and performances is bound to grow, there is no evidence that employment opportunities for the professional artist will increase. This is a situation which deprives Americans of the cultural opportunities they deserve and want, and discourages the development of creative talent.

I emphasize the importance of the professional artist because there is danger we may tend to accept the rich range of amateur activities which abound in our country as a substitute for the professional. Without the professional performer and the creative artist, the amateur declines and the vast audience is only partially served.

Art is no exception to the rule in human affairs—that of needing a stable and ample financial and institutional base. As education needs schools so art needs museums, actors and playwrights need theatres, and composers and musicians need opera companies and orchestras.

The Government has a responsibility to see that this important aspect of our lives is not neglected. The concept of the public welfare should reflect cultural as well as physical values, aesthetic as well as economic considerations. We have agencies of the Government which are concerned with the welfare and advancment of science and technology, of education, recreation, and health. We should now begin to give similar attention to the arts.

Specific problems and areas which I hope the Council will look into include the following:

I am particularly interested in the opportunities for young people to develop their gifts in the field of the arts and also to participate in an active cultural life. The Council will, I hope, examine the degree to which we are now meeting our responsibilities to young people in this area.

The Council should evaluate the many new forms and institutions which are developing. For example, the growth of state arts councils is significant, as is also the planning of community cultural centers in many cities and regions of the country.

The impact of various general governmental policies and programs on the arts is an area to which I hope the Council will give special attention. This includes such specific fields as tax laws, copyright laws, disposition of surplus property, public works and community development, public buildings, housing and urban renewal and others.

Public recognition of excellence in the arts is one effective way of giving encouragement. I am sure that the Council will want to give consideration to various possibilities in this field, including such forms of recognition as prizes, competitions, festivals, traveling tours and exhibitions.

Although the international cultural exchange program will not be a responsibility of the Council, the link between the vitality of our national cultural life and institutions and the success of our international programs is obvious. Our international programs are a direct reflection of our cultural achievements at home. I hope that the Council as it looks at the national cultural scene will consider its implications for our exchange programs.

The cultural life of the United States has at its best been varied, lively and decentralized. It has been supported—often with great generosity—by private patrons. I hope these characteristics will not change, but it seems well to assess how far the traditional sources of support meet the needs of the present and the near future. In giving form to this reassessment the President's Advisory Council on the Arts will be making a most important contribution to the national life.

STATE ARTS COUNCILS [4]

A growing number of state councils on the arts, to provide cultural opportunities in thousands of communities, are developing throughout the nation.

[4] From "Cultural Councils in 13 States Reflect an Upsurge of Interest," article by Milton Esterow, New York *Times* correspondent. New York *Times*. p 22. Je. 17, '63. © 1963 by The New York Times Company. Reprinted by permission.

Thirteen states, reflecting the national upsurge of interest in the arts, have such groups or plan to establish them, according to a survey by correspondents of the New York *Times*. Most of the councils have been formed in the last three years.

The councils are established by state legislatures to raise artistic standards and increase public exposure to all the arts. Some use state funds; others believe their main duty is to spur private patronage.

Stimulants to the councils have included President Kennedy's support of the arts, the rise in leisure time and an increasing repect for the role of the arts in a democratic society.

The states that have councils or plan them are New York, California, New Jersey, Connecticut, North Carolina, Michigan, Minnesota, Missouri, Ohio, Nebraska, Nevada, Washington and Virginia.

The councils vary from eleven members to one hundred and include leaders in the arts and in business.

The councils are stimulating arts activities locally, spurring the establishment of community groups and bringing live performances to people who have never had an opportunity to see them.

The Federal Advisory Council on the Arts, which President Kennedy established . . . [in June 1963], is expected to stimulate the council movement further.

In addition, Senator Jacob K. Javits [Republican] of New York and nine other senators . . . [in 1957] introduced a bill to grant up to $100,000 annually to states that have set up arts councils. . . . [This bill has since been killed; a new one has been introduced to replace it.—Ed.]

Some governors believe arts councils are not the responsibility of state governments. A number of states are still considered "cultural dust bowls."

A correspondent of the *Times* in Wisconsin reported: "No state program for support of the arts is contemplated here. People are struggling to convince the legislature that support of schools is a legitimate concern of the state."

One of the most significant contributions is being made by the New York State Council on the Arts, which was established three years ago at Governor Rockefeller's request.

The State Council has supported extended tours by organizations such as the Phoenix Theatre, the New York City Opera Company and the Buffalo Philharmonic. Its budget this year is $653,000.

John H. MacFadyen, the Council's executive director, said the Council received frequent requests from other states for information on setting up a program. He has prepared a guide outlining it.

"Each state has its particular artistic identity, and to this extent the programs that emerge will naturally differ," Mr. MacFadyen said.

In California, a bill to establish a fine arts commission is expected to pass the legislature. The measure, modeled on the New York State Council, is supported by Governor Edmund G. Brown.

Economy has influenced legislators to favor state assistance to the arts. Unions affected by the movie slump have argued' that state and community help for theatres would ease the Hollywood recession.

A Connecticut bill creating a state commission on the arts was signed into law on June 6 by Governor John Dempsey. The fifteen members will survey public and private cultural facilities in the state.

In New Jersey, Governor Richard J. Hughes recently named an eleven-man commission to study the arts. Members include the artist Ben Shahn and the playwright Selden Rodman. The state's first cultural center, which will cost $6 million is being built in Trenton. It is scheduled for completion next year.

For many years, North Carolina has considered support of the arts a vital concern. It owns and supports an art gallery in Raleigh and has contributed to the North Carolina Symphony Orchestra and subsidized outdoor dramas.

The General Assembly of North Carolina is considering a proposal to appropriate $325,000 for a school for the performing arts. . . .

In Missouri, Governor John M. Dalton named a twenty-five-member arts committee last December. A bill has been introduced in the legislature to create a Missouri Council on the Arts.

In Minnesota, the legislature has rejuvenated a lagging arts program that is sixty years old and has passed a State Arts Council bill.

Kentucky has a varied program—all instituted since 1960. Through the State Council on Public Higher Education, the state contracts with the Louisville Symphony Orchestra—at $50,000 annually—for performances at state colleges. The Lexington Little Symphony, backed by state funds, plays in small cities in cooperation with local civic groups.

The Kentucky Council of Performing Arts was recently set up.

Michigan established a cultural commission in 1960, and it now has one hundred members. William E. Stirton, a vice president of the University of Michigan who was serving as chairman, resigned in January, but he has continued his interest in the commission's activities.

Mr. Stirton said the commission had helped in establishing an artist in residence—a pianist—in Flint, and had encouraged communities to hold concerts and to develop arts centers.

In Virginia, the Barter Theatre at Abingdon has received an annual appropriation of $12,500 to $15,000 for many years.

The Virginia Museum of Fine Art in Richmond sends "artmobiles" with exhibitions to cities and towns. The museum helps plan programs through a statewide Confederation of the Arts established two years ago.

Nebraska created the Council for Nebraska's Cultural Resources in 1961. Its financing has come through private subscriptions and donations from individuals and corporations.

Dr. Walter Militzer, chairman of the Council and dean of the University of Nebraska's College of Arts and Science, said that "at this point the Council is a state coordinating agency for various local groups in cultural pursuits."

In Nevada, Governor Grant Sawyer is appointing a ten-member committee to determine possible steps toward a program. Dr. Craig Shepherd, head of the University of Nevada's Art Department, will be chairman of the council.

Washington created a state arts council in 1961, but only $2,000 has been appropriated for the next two years.

In Ohio, a bill to create an Ohio Arts Evaluation Commission to help in determining the role of state agencies in the growth of the arts is being considered in the legislature.

"It has not yet been conclusively determined that new government support for the arts will be truly effective," Mr. Mac-Fadyen said. "However, I believe that if this support develops with sound artistic objectives, a significant contribution to the arts in America will follow."

THE ARTIST IN AMERICA [5]

This day, devoted to the memory of Robert Frost, offers an opportunity for reflection which is prized by politicians as well as by others and even by poets. For Robert Frost was one of the granite figures of our time in America. He was supremely two things—an artist and an American.

A nation reveals itself not only by the men it produces but also by the men it honors, the men it remembers.

In America our heroes have customarily run to men of large accomplishments. But today this college and country honors a man whose contribution was not to our size but to our spirit; not to our political beliefs but to our insight; not to our self-esteem, but to our self-comprehension.

In honoring Robert Frost we therefore can pay honor to the deepest sources of our national strength. That strength takes many forms and the most obvious forms are not always the most significant.

The men who create power make an indispensable contribution to the nation's greatness. But the men who question power make a contribution just as indispensable, especially when that questioning is disinterested.

For they determine whether we use power or power uses us. Our national strength matters; but the spirit which informs and controls our strength matters just as much. This was the special significance of Robert Frost.

He brought an unsparing instinct for reality to bear on the platitudes and pieties of society. His sense of the human tragedy fortified him against self-deception and easy consolation.

[5] From address by the late President John F. Kennedy, delivered at Amherst College, October 26, 1963, on the dedication of the Robert Frost Library. Text from the New York *Times.* p 87. O. 27, '63.

"I have been," he wrote, "one acquanted with the night."

And because he knew the midnight as well as the high noon, because he understood the ordeal as well as the triumph of the human spirit, he gave his age strength with which to overcome despair.

At bottom he held a deep faith in the spirit of man. And it's hardly an accident that Robert Frost coupled poetry and power. For he saw poetry as the means of saving power from itself.

When power leads man toward arrogance, poetry reminds him of his limitations. When power narrows the areas of man's concern, poetry reminds him of the richness and diversity of his existence. When power corrupts, poetry cleanses.

For art establishes the basic human truths which must serve as the touchstones of our judgment. The artist, however faithful to his personal vision of reality, becomes the last champion of the individual mind and sensibility against an intrusive society and an officious state.

The great artist is thus a solitary figure. He has, as Frost said, "a lover's quarrel with the world." In pursuing his perceptions of reality he must often sail against the currents of his time. This is not a popular role.

If Robert Frost was much honored during his lifetime, it was because a good many preferred to ignore his darker truths.

Yet in retrospect we see how the artist's fidelity has strengthened the fiber of our national life. If sometimes our great artists have been the most critical of our society it is because their sensitivity and their concern for justice, which must motivate any true artist, makes him aware that our nation falls short of its highest potential.

I see little of more importance to the future of our country and our civilization than full recognition of the place of the artist. If art is to nourish the roots of our culture, society must set the artist free to follow his vision wherever it takes him.

We must never forget that art is not a form of propaganda, it is a form of truth. And as Mr. [Archibald] MacLeish once remarked of poets, "There is nothing worse for our trade than to be in style."

In free society art is not a weapon and it does not belong to the sphere of polemics and ideology. Artists are not engineers of the soul.

It may be different elsewhere. But democratic society—in it— the highest duty of the writer, the composer, the artist is to remain true to himself and to let the chips fall where they may.

In serving his vision of the truth the artist best serves his nation. And the nation which disdains the mission of art invites the fate of Robert Frost's hired man—"the fate of having nothing to look backward to with pride and nothing to look forward to with hope."

I look forward to a great future for America—a future in which our country will match its military strength with our moral restraint, its wealth with our wisdom, its power with our purpose.

I look forward to an America which will not be afraid of grace and beauty, which will protect the beauty of our natural environment, which will preserve the great old American houses and squares and parks of our national past and which will build handsome and balanced cities for our future.

I look forward to an America which will reward achievement in the arts as we reward achievement in business or statecraft.

I look forward to an America which will steadily raise the standards of artistic accomplishment and which will steadily enlarge cultural opportunities for all of our citizens.

And I look forward to an America which commands respect throughout the world not only for its strength but for its civilization as well.

And I look forward to a world which will be safe not only for democracy and diversity but also for personal distinction.

Robert Frost was often skeptical about projects for human improvement. Yet I do not think he would disdain this hope. As he wrote during the uncertain days of the Second War:

> Take human nature altogether since time began, . . .
> And it must be a little more in favor of man,
> Say a fraction of one per cent at the very least, . . .
> Our hold on the planet wouldn't have so increased.

Because of Mr. Frost's life and work, because of the life and work of this college, our hold on this planet has increased.

IV. AMERICAN CULTURE IN THE SIXTIES: A SURVEY

EDITOR'S INTRODUCTION

A whole is made up of the sum of its parts, but the parts are not necessarily equal. The American cultural explosion of the sixties is the sum of its individual arts—painting and sculpture, literature and drama, music, ballet, and in this age of the mass media one must also include motion pictures and television. A close examination of the state of these individual arts reveals a curious imbalance; some of them are flourishing while others seem to be wasting away. Granted that to some degree the health of the arts is in the eye of the beholder. In television, for example, one can hopefully cite individual "quality" programs, college credit courses, and whole channels devoted to cultural and educational features. Or one can switch the dial to an interminable succession of trash, vulgarity, and mediocrity never before produced in America in such quantity or distributed to such wide audiences. Two views on the cultural manifestations of American television are therefore reprinted in this section in order to represent the balance fairly.

On the health of the American motion picture there is not even a significant division of opinion. It is sick, perhaps not fatally; but, as Arthur Mayer points out in his article here, if it survives it will be only as the result of radical changes in the industry. The American theatre in the sixties also presents a gloomy picture. So complex indeed is its condition that one must examine it from at least four different angles—the commercial Broadway theatre (which in 1962-1963, according to the New York *Times* of May 24, 1963, had its most disastrous season in memory, with a loss to its investors of more than half a million dollars), the off-Broadway theatre in New York, the regional-provincial theatre in the rest of the United States, and the drama itself, the plays which are being currently written and produced. Literature too does not appear to be flourishing in the sixties. Hemingway and Faulkner died within a year of each other in

1961-1962, many years after the publication of their most significant works, and not a single major novelist has emerged in their place. Fiction has in general been relegated to second place or lower with the reading public. Poetry offers a brighter outlook, but no amount of cultural explosion has materially increased the audience for it.

It has been suggested that ours is not particularly a literary or a verbal age. But it is certainly a visual and aural one. Painting, sculpture, and the graphic arts are thriving. The number of Sunday painters, museum visitors, and art collectors may not be an accurate gauge of a cultural renaissance, but, as Katharine Kuh points out in her article, American taste at last appears to be coming of age. Serious music similarly has been enjoying attention and respect such as it has never had before. Great "centers" of opera and symphonic music, once confined to New York, Chicago, and San Francisco, are now being built throughout the country. From the lofty performing halls to the home hi-fi sets, America seems to be listening to more good music more enthusiastically, more appreciatively, and more knowledgeably than ever. But again a closer examination reveals alarming gaps in our knowledge and appreciation, especially our failure to support the new and experimental in music.

Music, however, has always been a major, if popularly neglected, part of our nation's culture. More remarkable in the 1960's is the rapidly changing image of the ballet. Once an art form appreciated only by visiting Europeans and a small group of native eccentrics and bohemians, it is now developing into a popular and relatively lucrative entertainment medium. Dancers are still underpaid and, in contrast to performers in other fields, ignored by the general public. But, as Allen Hughes reports in his article, more people are spending more money to see serious dancing than ever before in our history. Dance connoisseurs are few, but the support of a mass audience is a guarantee—probably the only guarantee—that the serious dance will remain alive.

Mass support is indeed the only guarantee for the future of all the arts. In America in the 1960's there is a mass public, eager and educable, for culture in any form. Whether that public will be raised to the level of the arts or the arts reduced to the level of the public is perhaps the greatest challenge that American culture faces today.

ART IN AMERICA IN 1962 [1]

Recently an American painter forced automobile tires to substitute for his brush, resolutely driving back and forth over his canvas. More disheartening than this contrived act was the prominence given to it by a popular magazine that prides itself on cultural awareness. Another painter who presumably values expediency over privacy has been widely publicized for an equally novel, if less mechanical, technique. He covers a nude woman with paint and, this time, it is her body—not an automobile—that rolls over the canvas.

Innovations catch on overnight. There is now a sudden enthusiasm for so-called comic-strip paintings. Usually devoid of invention, these over-large copies (and *copies* they are) literally reproduce and enlarge familiar comic-strip scenes. Touted as the new American folk art, they are selling with breathless speed. When one thinks of Léger's authentic use of folk art, his ability to transform it into new, often bold and witty compositions, one realizes that without deliberate translation art cannot exist.

Somewhat less exhibitionistic than these chic novelties, but no less tedious are the innumerable empty canvases covered with only one color. More than forty years ago the Russian, Kasimir Malevich, painted his famous "Suprematist Composition: White on White," proving that much can be done with little and making the current "one-color men" seem awkwardly dated; for as yet they have added little or nothing to his definitive statement.

Today, any technique accented by a single easily labeled characteristic is apt to be speedily and enthusiastically acclaimed. Why seasoned collectors are so willingly snared is a provocative question. Surely they must realize that great discoveries scarcely spring full blown from every hopeful neophyte. However, it is not experimentation I am deploring; it is the *lack* of it, the shallow imitation of invention.

The influence of publicity became exceptionally clear recently when a reputable national art organization admitted that its top executive job demanded promotional experience more than a knowledge of art. Also symptomatic is the number of private

[1] From article by Katharine Kuh, art critic and contributing editor, *Saturday Review.* *Saturday Review.* 45:30A-30P. S. 8, '52. Reprinted by permission.

collectors who maintain personal public relations counsels. One might expect that those whose fortunes do not depend on popularity polls would be the last to expose themselves to public glare. But now, as the possession of art becomes a more and more reliable passport to social success, it is only the very innocent who fail to recognize its power. Our museums and even the White House tend to encourage this situation in their zeal for private support. . . .

No discussion of the fine arts is possible today without mention of the fantastic prices that paintings and sculpture are bringing at auction—and without equal mention of the fantastic antics surrounding these events. We seem to have read more about Mr. James Rorimer's slight twitch of the eyebrow, when as director of the Metropolitan Museum he acquired Rembrandt's "Aristotle Contemplating the Bust of Homer" . . . at the Parke-Bernet sale, than we have read about the picture itself. No one denies that this is a splendid painting, but the publicity accompanying its purchase focused on price almost to the exclusion of art. The gigantic figure of $2.3 million was used, it would seem, as bait to lure thousands of curious visitors. If one assumes that mere exposure to a work of art is enough, then these methods are less open to debate, but I question whether the throngs pouring into the Metropolitan for a hectic look at a costly painting have taken much of value away with them.

The majority, I am sure, did not know that for many years two equally distinguished, possibly more distinguished, examples of Rembrandt's work have been hanging only a few blocks away at the Frick Collection. These, the brilliant "Polish Rider" . . . and the moving "Self-Portrait," . . . make one doubt whether New York needed another masterpiece by this artist as much as did the underbidder, Cleveland's Museum of Art (particularly since the Metropolitan already has some thirty examples). The entire transaction brings up any number of questions. Should American public-service institutions be pitted against one another in ruthless competition? Isn't the final loser the public? For even though most of our museums are privately endowed, they presumably serve public needs and constantly appeal to this same public for financial help.

A further sign of the capitulation of museums to price-glamour publicity appeared recently in a newspaper item about a rare

Tiepolo painting. This time the story came from that stronghold of conservatism, Boston. To quote, "The most expensive painting ever bought by the Boston Museum of Fine Arts went on display today in the museum's Rotunda. . . . Perry T. Rathbone, museum director, said the museum had insured the work for about $250,000. He did not reveal the purchase price, but said it was the highest ever paid by the museum."

In the past, museums were proud of acquiring great masterpieces for little money; it took knowledge, a nimble eye, and a poker face. But now, bowing to the press, museum eyes seem more geared to Wall Street than to aesthetics. It is scarcely surprising that art thefts are frequent and prices steeply inflated.

Willem Sandberg, Director of the Stedlijk Museum in Amsterdam, may have hit the nail on the head when he recently expressed the opinion that "all American museums suffer from the trustee system. Once you have confidence in a director, you must give him freedom. And confidence naturally implies that a director is a specialist in art." But this unfortunately is what many top museum men are not; they are more and more being chosen for their administrative ability, their financial acumen, their charm, their agreeable willingness to rubber-stamp trustee decisions. In addition, art museum trustees are thinking increasingly of their institutions as business enterprises, and of themselves as art specialists, a hazardous and ironic inversion that leads to incompetent behavior on both levels. . . .

Though many of art's present difficulties result from gigantism—from bigger and bigger prices, bigger and bigger museums, bigger and bigger exhibitions, bigger and bigger works of art, yet I must confess that during the last year some of the largest exhibits were the best, some of the largest paintings the most rewarding. And it is only fair to note that certain momentous exhibitions were sponsored by our largest museums. Indeed, often what we most deplore paradoxically turns up in the credit column.

One thinks immediately of the superb Chinese Art Treasures lent by the Republic of China, . . . a comprehensive and unforgettable survey that traveled to several major American museums. In this show the early scroll paintings, among the most civilized works of art ever produced, were mute reminders of Oriental profundity. Nature, depicted as all pervasive, is endowed in these paintings with supernatural grandeur, revealing man appropriately dwarfed by the elements. Fortunate were the many Americans who experienced this extraordinary exhibition, where flawless technique served an art of unparalleled wisdom.

Fortunate, also, were those who saw a small show of monumental collages by Henri Matisse. If the Chinese paintings were a supreme expression of man's mastery over the flesh, so also, in a more personal way, were Matisse's joyous mural-like cut-and-pasted gouaches. When the artist made these compositions toward the end of his life, he was ill and unable to work at his easel, but his inventive vision, his feeling for explosive line and color were not to be quenched. Triumphing over his infirmities, Matisse created a group of large painted, cutout, and pasted gouaches of such brilliance, gaiety, and economy as to rank with his greatest works. . . .

For American artists, critics and laymen, the Matisse show was a revelation. Not one wasted line, not one hint of hesitation burdened these compositions, which were virtually conceived with the edges of a scissors. It is difficult to identify such consummate control and dazzling color, such optimism and vitality, with a man well over eighty. Surpassing even Renoir, who in his late years tied brushes to his wrists and painted from a wheel chair, Matisse, likewise confined to a wheel chair, proved once again that for artists old age is not a handicap.

And two other octogenarians, this time Americans, confirm the same judgment. Hans Hofmann and Edward Hopper, diametrically opposed as painters, both seem at the peak of their power today. In the section devoted to American art at the Seattle Fair, Hofmann . . . [was] by far the oldest exhibitor; yet his two canvases . . . [sang] out with such luminous vibrancy that they . . . . [made] the adjacent works of younger followers appear tepid. One of these canvases called "Olive Grove" was painted in 1961 after a trip to Italy. Characteristically, it evokes the artist's feelings in the presence of nature, but in no way documents a specific scene.

On the other hand, Edward Hopper's "Second-Story Sunlight," recently acquired by the Whitney Museum of American Art, is based on more easily recognizable elements, though it also is an imaginary scene. The deliberate spontaneity and exuberance of Hofmann is here replaced by calculated restraint. Every window shade, every shadow is almost mathematically determined. In Hopper's words, there is "a sort of elation about sunlight on the upper part of a house." Though one composition blazes with color and erupts with pigment, the other, stressing contrasts of light, denies all surface texture; though one composition is non-objective and the other naturalistic, they are both basically abstract. Hopper is less interested in his figures and house than in the way light transforms them, and Hofmann's color surprises suggest but do not describe his personal emotions. Both men are authentic pioneers of modern American painting.

One other traveling exhibition made history this season. The Thomas Eakins show may have failed for certain modern eyes because of its solid solemnity and stolid color, but, for me, this painter towers above his nineteenth century American contemporaries, not because of his uncompromising honesty (true, also, sometimes of them), but because of his uncanny ability to interpret his own times and his own country. This was the era when Europe called the plays; yet Eakins called his own. If his interest was more in the particular than the general, he was nonetheless able to project with searching perception the dry, unpretentious, forthright quality of the America he knew—an America fast disappearing. Eakins is remembered for his portraits, sport scenes, and realistic paintings of surgical operations, and for the unvarnished insight he brought to these often prosaic subjects. . . .

There have been other fine exhibitions—Calder, Henry Moore, Gonzalez, Dubuffet, Léger—all accepted modern "old masters." When it comes to recent large group shows, the emphasis has been almost exclusively on painters and sculptors backed by New York galleries—many of whom too often seem unseasoned, untested, and immature. No one can accuse the present art market of ignoring the young. However, there are any number of able painters and sculptors not living within reach of the East Coast who are seldom featured in official shows. One cannot help wondering why exhibition directors travel extensively to Europe and even to Asia, while yet neglecting some of the largest art centers in their own country.

During occasional trips I have come on interesting painters and sculptors, artists like Bryan Wilson and Richard Bowman of California, Evelyn Statsinger of Chicago, James Fitzgerald of

Seattle, Joseph Goto (particularly his monumental metal sculpture) of Ann Arbor, none of whom is represented as a rule in large national exhibitions. And rest assured—there are many others. In Michigan, for example, an excellent group of watercolorists is well worth watching. That the New York school has produced certain formidable men of great stature does not justify the neglect of promising American artists living elsewhere.

Still the wealth of art galleries and museums in and near New York City is a prodigious, not to say healthy, indication of public interest. One Sunday last May, I counted in the New York *Times* no less than seventeen public institutions featuring art shows, some of major importance.

Moreover, the high performance of certain smaller specialized institutions like Asia House and the Museum of Primitive Art in New York, the peerless Phillips Collection in Washington, and the George Eastman House in Rochester are, let us hope, clues to the future. University and college art museums also, as a rule, are comfortably limited in size and ambition. With them scholarship often compensates for modest funds, acquisitions reflecting knowledge more than public pressure. And, in addition, many colleges and universities are organizing excellent art festivals designed to serve not only the student body but the entire surrounding community. These festivals are now spreading even to high schools and grammar schools. One of the best I have seen takes place annually at the New Canaan, Connecticut, Public High School. This lively show, covering only the work of students, includes prints, paintings, ceramics, drawings, collages, sculpture, and design. Here one senses the influence of perceptive teachers who have obviously stressed content above technique. The work throughout shows a touching freshness and genuine intensity rarely found in the average self-conscious teen-ager.

Speaking of students, another promising omen occurred this spring at Columbia University. There, and also at Princeton University and Trinity College, students have organized against what they consider bad architectural designs planned for their respective campuses. The Columbia group was particularly incensed over a projected new School of Business to be called Uris Hall. The designs, extremely dull and pedestrian, recall dreary Fascist architecture from Mussolini's day. One student wisely observed: "The building should have some image relating to the students who work in it. This building looks no different than a post office or a branch office of an insurance company." William Platt, a member of the University's Advisory Committee on Architecture and Planning, was quoted in the *Times* as having replied: "It should not be the kind of building the architecture students have in mind. Rather, it should be a nonentity, an efficient building that fits in." Somehow $7 million seems a lot to spend on a nonentity.

One need only compare the small, wonderfully inventive Roofless Church of New Harmony, Indiana, to appreciate why architecture must relate visually and emotionally as well as functionally to the purpose it serves. Philip Johnson, who designed the church, and Jacques Lipchitz, who made the sculpture for it, obviously worked in close harmony to produce a chapel reflecting both the religious freedom and the Utopian philosophy that have distinguished New Harmony's history. To be sure, sympathetic church sponsorship of art and architecture is not new. In the Middle Ages and the Renaissance, it was standard practice, but during the past two decades in both Europe and the United States, a rebirth of the same interest has produced a body of notable modern church architecture. Only recently Marcel Breuer's Abbey Church in Collegeville, Minnesota, was dedicated. Here this architect designed a whole complex of buildings highly modern in character, but nonetheless reflecting the religious life and needs of the Benedictine brothers for whom it was built.

We also have big business to thank for other evidences of present-day progressive cooperation in the arts. The Chase Manhattan Bank, the Inland Steel Company in Chicago, the Seagram Building, the airport in St. Louis—these and many other business organizations are imaginatively combining modern architecture and art. Today even factories are commissioning painters and sculptors, as industry fast becomes one of art's most liberal patrons. And the best architects, too, are increasingly collaborating with contemporary sculptors to introduce works of art into the daily lives of our communities.

In addition, New York State under the leadership of art-conscious Governor Nelson Rockefeller . . . established an exemplary Council of the Arts, the first of its kind in the country. With the sole aim of promoting cultural welfare, this organization has an enviable record and may, let us hope, act as a spur to other states and to the Federal Government. Because it has concentrated heavily on the needs of smaller institutions, implementing their art programs with exhibitions and services specifically adapted to their communities, the council has already proved invaluable. Not limited to the fine arts, this group likewise sponsors state-wide theatre, music, ballet, and opera programs often experimental in character.

Another refreshing development is the increasing number of modest and informative art publications. Those many costly coffee-table art books that prize jazzed-up color reproductions above thoughtful texts are at last being challenged by a group of smaller, well-edited volumes (usually in connected series), where words are not merely perfunctory space fillers.

Priced within comfortable reach of students and the general public, these books are also frequently well illustrated. I particularly recommend a compact series called The Complete Library of World Art, each volume devoted to a single celebrated master. Reproductions of the artist's entire *œuvre* are followed by excellent enlarged details and accurate, intelligent information. Though somewhat more routine, the Student Series of Great Artists is also notable for its color reproductions and its clear, sympathetic language. Nor is architecture overlooked. A series called the Great Ages of World Architecture publishes condensed volumes devoted to individual periods in the history of architecture. Again the books are written by specialists who are concerned with authentic, concise interpretations, a happy relief from the plethora of phony words that envelop art today. . . .

And, finally, one cannot draw up a balance sheet on the arts in America today without saluting the White House, if only for Mrs. Kennedy's serious concern with restoring authentic furniture, sculpture, and paintings to this historic landmark. Already several fine colonial canvases by such distinguished artists as Rembrandt Peale and John Trumbull have been acquired. One of the noblest acquisitions, however, is not by an American but of an important American. A "Portrait of Benjamin Franklin" painted from life by the Scotch artist David Martin shows the sitter at sixty years of age. This uncompromising likeness has none of the frothy artificiality sometimes associated with the eighteenth century. It is memorable for a frank integrity that echoes the personality of its renowned subject. . . .

From a long-range view, American taste does indeed seem to be slowly coming of age as its sights veer from "Grand Rapids modern" to Charles Eames, from neo-Gothic to Eero Saarinen, from Rockwell Kent to Mark Tobey. But in order fully to come of age, the art profession as a whole must face up to its own peculiar brand of "juvenile delinquency."

PURSUIT OF THE REAL [2]

More than any of the other art forms, the novel is expected to reflect the world around it—the way people live, the things they hope for or fear. In theory at least, poetry idealizes us, drama heroizes us, but the novel shows us as we are. This assumption goes back to Cervantes' conception of the Don and Sancho, gained momentum in eighteenth century England, in the novels of Defoe, Fielding and Richardson, and reached full strength in the last century with Jane Austen, Stendhal, Balzac, Dickens, Flaubert, Thackeray and George Eliot.

Evidently, after the dislocations of our age, we no longer make this claim about the novel's hold on reality in the same way. The obvious question now is: what reality? Even, what is reality? Are we talking about the same thing that occupied Dickens and George Eliot, much less Cervantes and Defoe? With the nature of reality itself in question, the major novels of the twentieth century have not unusually been metaphysical, from Conrad's concern with the function of illusions to Mann's preoccupation with sickness and health. In the pursuit of the real, Conrad and Mann, together with Lawrence, Proust, Kafka, Faulkner and Joyce, have greatly extended novelistic reality and directed us to recognize the multiplicity of experience and the protean nature of life. We have come to view the world not as a stable place but as a web of overlapping illusions, as an ever-expanding function of memory, as a manifestation of irrational responses and perverse desires, and as an obstacle course in which man is forever trapped. This powerful demonstration of uncertainty and mystery has been the substance of the major writers;

[2] From article by Frederick R. Karl, associate professor of English, City College of the City University of New York. *The Nation.* 194:345-9. Ap. 21, '62. Reprinted by permission.

while the reputable minor ones—both in England and the United States—continue in the Victorian main stream and reflect a relatively stable world.

Paradoxically, however, most people live as though stability were not only possible but already present. Their public lives, as well as their private (despite the high divorce rate), are based on ambitions, goals, continuity. They strive and seek; they hope to find; they build, and then settle in; they raise large families— in itself a sign of optimism and a mark of relative security. They struggle for better positions, for more money, for higher status. No matter what their private fears, their lives are founded on more than mere survival, in fact, on attainable self-gratification.

There would seem to be, then, a sharp contradiction between the way most people see themselves and the way the novel reflects life. There might even seem to be real deception, leading to the charge often found in the popular press that the novelist mirrors a world that people never made. Editorial writers and popular critics point insistently to the fact that the contents of most "important" novels are excessively violent and eccentric, hope- lessly tragic and unrepresentative of a people who are forward- looking and basically optimistic. Such views lose sight of the whole tradition of American fiction, which, if nothing else, has been pessimistic, eccentric, dark and violent.

The current American novel continues this tradition, although at the same time it curiously does reflect many aspects of a real society in which people hold jobs, marry, have children and maintain their individuality. In other areas as well—in the ambivalent relationship of the American to religion, for example, and to the demands of his society—the novelist is "true" to what surrounds him. Even Faulkner's Gothic distortions occur in a recognizable world of fact. This attempt to probe everyday society, with no matter how bizarre a method, is generally more apparent in the current American novelists (Bellow, Malamud, Heller, Bourjaily, Styron, Salinger, Katherine Anne Porter, Sigal, Wallant—to mention only those who have recently published books) than it is in recent continental fiction (Beckett, Butor, Robbe-Grillet, Moravia) or even among the English (Murdoch, Golding, Greene, Durrell), with the exceptions of C. P. Snow, Alan Sillitoe and Angus Wilson. . . .

For the American novelist, people and their immediate lives count a great deal. Things, in fact, exist only to be put to use. They do not dominate or overpower the characters; when people are overwhelmed, it is by other people, by the huge block of society which makes them victims. Thus, for Heller, in *Catch-22*, and Malamud, in *A New Life*, man is victimized, and it remains for him to seek his salvation alone, even when personal salvation may mean a rejection of human solidarity. There is, here, almost a complete break with the social novel of the 1930's which saw in united action the way to transcend individual difficulties. Yossarian, of *Catch-22*, decides that self-preservation is more important than the insane demands of his commanding officer, although he deserts only after he is sure he has done as much as can be expected of the individual. He is a modern-day Crusoe who recognizes that the needs of the individual must, at some point, pre-empt the social need.

In *A New Life*—the title ironically recalls Dante's—Malamud's S. Levin must find a new self, at whatever cost of chaos left in his wake. In Styron's *Set This House on Fire*, Cass Kinsolving expiates his sordid past by murdering Mason Flagg whom he sees as an evil force, a social menace. In George Mandel's much neglected *The Breakwater*, Zale finds in rebellion an entire way of life, although, ironically, it also leads to his death. Bellow's Henderson, like a Lawrentian hero, tries to transcend the whole social order to resurrect his soul. With his lion in tow and the Persian-speaking child clutched to his chest, he finds an inner peace that somehow makes war, strife and ambition meaningless. In Katherine Anne Porter's *Ship of Fools*, people on the edge of a world catastrophe enjoy their food, sex and nastiness to one another—qualities that preserve them as individuals.

Involved though they are with the urgency of self-preservation and the needs of the individual, there are, nevertheless, few major American novels presently concerned with ambition and the will toward power—the qualities that occupy C. P. Snow. *The Affair*, number eight in his "Strangers and Brothers" series, shows Snow still interested in careers: (say) a Royal Society membership, an important book or piece of research, an advancement in administrative power, a high post in government service, even a Nobel Prize. Snow's "reality" is that of our overt lives, whereas most of the Americans—and some of the French—are concerned with dissecting the interior life where anxieties and conflicts are more important than the individual's actual behavior. . . .

For the contemporary American writer, there is no such central concern with work and duty; his main characters must function in a real world of dislocation. For Heller and Bourjaily (Quincy in *Confessions of a Spent Youth*), man is at war; his "career" is simply to stay alive and allay his fears with sex and alcohol. Bellow's Henderson has already made his money and is now free to remake himself. Updike's Harry Angstrom (in *Rabbit, Run*) leaves his wife and job (as a Woolworth barker) and floats free, relatively guiltless, to try to be himself unencumbered by responsibilities or duties. Salinger's Franny and Zooey are perpetual adolescents free to contemplate Zen or anything else that catches their imagination. Even Malamud's Levin, who tries to resurrect his soul through college teaching, fails miserably and by the last chapter had drifted free of his career.

In these American novels, work has become, in fact, almost a taboo. The protagonist rarely identifies with his job, and he is antipathetic toward those who are overly committed to theirs. Just as the steady worker sees his free-floating colleague as a potential menace, so does the floater see his plugging colleague as priggish, self-righteous, somehow dishonest and phony for pursuing goals that are ultimately meaningless. It is very important for the American writers that his protagonist be "cool" or "hip," in contradistinction (say) to the earnestness of Snow's Lewis Eliot. . . . To be cool means that the individual first satisfies himself; that he rejects institutions, traditions and conventions; that he works out his own secular morality. He has a code, but it is unwritten, usually unspoken. It may be revealed by a gesture or by silence. He becomes the last bastion of sanity in an insane world.

This element of the American experience is engrained in the tradition. While the central character remains alienated to almost everything outside himself, his struggle is to avoid self-alienation. He must obsessively pursue his identity which, not bestowed at birth, has still to be won. That is a "real" view of society and survival, although one not involving civilian defense, unemployment, automation, the threat of communism or imminent destruction by atomic warfare. Curiously, it coincides quite closely with the views of a good part of society, which is apathetic to most outside threats except those that are immediately unavoidable.

We must make a clear distinction between official pronouncements and private lives. Opinion polls repeatedly show that people are not responsive to the big ideas and the big threats to survival, but to the day-to-day menaces which somehow loom larger. It is just this world that the American novelist describes—though he works through distortions that act as a comment on the given community. Tolstoy's naturalness of content and style cannot serve writers concerned with fragmentation and instability. While Tolstoy agreed with Shakespeare that ripeness is all, the current writer does not even seek wholeness. Instead, he asks, "What is my name? How did I get it? Do I want to keep it? And what threats are constantly present to destroy it?" A man now has to prove himself, not by being accomplished or successful, but simply by being a man.

Further, although the quality of a man's life may often be empty or aimless, the possibility of resurrection (on a small scale) is almost always present. His "escape" may be a mixed blessing, but it is nevertheless an escape into an area where the self can be pursued and individuality can be reaffirmed: thus, Yossarian's desertion, Levin's flight from Cascadia College, Cass Kinsolving's murder of Mason Flagg, Quincy's attempt to efface his past in sexual adventures, the pursuit of "experience" by various Mailer protagonists, Henderson's rebirth in darkest Africa where even Kurtz would have feared to go, Rabbit Angstrom's ducking of responsibility in order to find some "true self." The point is dramatized tersely and effectively in Peter Matthiessen's *Raditzer,* wherein Charlie Stark discovers an entirely new dimension of self under the perverse influence of Raditzer. Clearly, there is no single reality, no single self, no single life. . . .

The American writer moves . . . in space; he covers vast distances, whole continents, rather than periods of time. He slights history. His protagonists do not age in time so much as they suddenly become old after traveling thousands of miles. They remain, usually, young enough to take on any available female, to experience a new adventure, to pursue what they hope will be a new sensation or pleasure. Their quest is a spatial one; and it is in space, rather than time, that the American writer weaves whatever continuity he achieves.

Not unusually, then, the American writer is less concerned with love than with lust—for love takes time, while lust takes only a place: the back seat of a car or, in an affluent society, the girl's apartment. In space, the direct approach to sex is important, while in time, a courtship is possible, even necessary. The novelist "realistically" assumes that sex will give only temporary relief, that joy or happiness is not an expectation but only a chance by-product. The protagonist can always move on. By car or airplane he can forage the country for sex, planting his seed before drifting away to harvest someone else's work. This is how our creative writers see us: as a people for whom love is almost unobtainable, for whom sexual intercourse is a form of escape or quest, and for whom there is really nothing else to do but float to the next adventure. . . .

Katherine Anne Porter, for instance, in *Ship of Fools* sees society in terms of a voyage, during which every relationship is fleeting and love or friendship impossible. Everyone is on the run—the Americans as well as the Germans and Spanish—to pursue false dreams, to fulfill vain hopes, to continue to be nasty and selfish. There are, unfortunately, no alternatives. And for Clancy Sigal, in *Going Away,* movement is all, from the title itself through the last paragraph, in which the narrator leaves America for Europe. As a space novel, *Going Away* is almost a paradigm: here there are no lasting connections, everything is change (for the worse). Even the left-wing movement which had once fiercely engaged Sigal's narrator has gone false and sour, now a mockery of its former excitement. What, then, is left besides flight? Sigal writes:

> I see no salvation in personal relationships, in political action, or in any job I might undertake in society. Everything in me cries out that we are meaningless pieces of paste. . . . That man is alone and can only relieve but not redeem his loneliness. That, to the extent we try to deny this—and most things in America aim at denying this—to that extent we participate in a living lie which must corrupt if not destroy us.

Updike's Rabbit is also indicative of this need to move on in order obsessively to seek one's self, to relieve one's loneliness. The title suggests the content. Rabbit lives in space; even his years as a great basketball player denote the need to run. For basketball—the most popular of American sports—is a game of back and forth, of almost constant movement. As Rabbit runs from his wife and children, so he runs from himself: his failure to accept responsibility for them, no matter how trying they are, is his failure to accept self-responsibility. Rabbit runs, for that is the nature of a rabbit, an adequate but depressing symbol of the free-wheeling American male on the make, perhaps of the American in his national and world role.

These novelists . . . reflect a reality that balks resolution. The pressures are too great, man's separation from others and from himself too immense, the important issues too distant. The power of the human will to overcome problems, even to create happiness—what every ninetenth century novelist took for granted—is now in serious doubt, and only popular minor novelists like Wouk, Sloan Wilson and Ruark seriously believe in it. The major writers continue to reflect the world that Kafka caught forty years ago, in which man's unconscious fears have become more momentous than his conscious plans and hopes. . . .

The tensions and conflicts that contemporary novelists reflect may often seem radically different from our own personal ones, but like their major predecessors, these writers are concerned with the timeless questions of guilt, conscience, responsibility and, ultimately, man's essence. The most impressive of the current novelists seem to indicate that the cultivation of self-responsibility—with or without a sense of guilt—is one's only hope in a world that has veered out of control. Without injuring others and without prostituting some dim ideal of behavior, one is obligated to save oneself rather than probe a meaningless fate; and this "solution," depressing though it is, is generally acceptable to the American and English writer, as well as to his more despairing continental coevals. By some ironic twist, the novel which began with Defoe's fierce sense of human individuality has come down to us, almost 350 years later, with its stress upon the individual as the sole hope in a dislocated age. As such, despite its vast changes, the novel mirrors the way people live and feel, no matter how they may publicly argue differently. Man may not be important enough to be tragic, but in the long run he and his inner life are the only things that count. On this point, even the most despairing of writers seem to agree.

POETRY'S SILVER AGE: AN IMPROBABLE DIALOGUE [3]

YOUNG MAN: But why then does everybody complain about the state of poetry today? Except for poets themselves and would-be poets, who reads poetry anyhow?

POET: Despite what I've said before, the audience is larger than you think, much larger than the cash register indicates. I've already mentioned the anthologies that are devoured annually in the tens of thousands by our schools and colleges. The new paperback editions of contemporary poets, particularly those issued by The City Lights Pocket Bookshop of San Francisco and by Grove Press of New York, have already blasted all the traditional publishers' preconceptions about the limitations of the market. Any librarian will tell you that books and periodicals of verse are in constant circulation. *Poetry* of Chicago, I hear, has doubled its subscription list in recent years. Furthermore, a published poet is sure to find friends of his work in almost any city in the country, and these readers of poetry are extraordinarily sympathetic and generous.

The ordeal of the artist, of which we hear so much, is real enough, God knows, but so are his joys. The poets of my acquaintance are doing precisely what they want to do and what they believe they do best. Nobody had to twist their arm to make poets out of them. And there's something else to be said. Despite all the lamentations about the state of poetry in America today, the general level of quality, I dare say, is higher than it ever has been in our literary history. It isn't a Golden Age for several obvious reasons, including the absence of one or two monumental geniuses in their prime to consolidate the poetic energies of the age; but it may very well be a Silver Age. I don't envy the lot of the anthologist of the future when he tries to cut the lyrics representing this century down to what he considers a reasonable number. My guess is—my wild guess, if you will—that only the Elizabethan Age will make a better showing.

[3] From "American Poetry's Silver Age," article by Stanley Kunitz, Pulitzer Prize-winning poet and editor. *Harper's Magazine.* 219:173-9. O. 59. Reprinted by permission.

EBB TIDE IN THE THEATRE [4]

Postwar evidence of loss of energy in American dramatic writing is occasionally contradicted by the sudden eruption of some vital new play or production. The English stage in the same period rarely has displayed such vitality, at least not until 1956 when John Osborne's *Look Back in Anger* startled London with its scattered grapeshot. But despite intermittent explosions, which have continued to occur right up to 1960 with Lillian Hellman's *Toys in the Attic*, the American theatre on the whole has not delivered the punch which has been its main distinction ever since 1920.

Optimists could be encountered at the beginning of the fifties. Professor Oscar James Campbell of Columbia seemed confident that what our theatre was losing in power it was gaining in sensibility. In the opinion of those who preferred the early plays of Tennessee Williams, William Inge (*Come Back, Little Sheba*), and Carson McCullers (*The Member of the Wedding*) to the unwieldy sociology of the preceding generation, our theatre was gaining also in finesse. Regret for the passing of the old earnestness was voiced only by a small number of unreconstructed middle-aged liberals. To be a passionate adherent of almost any point of view or to be forthrightly critical of the status quo was certain to make the playwright suspect. If he was not labeled as politically subversive, literary circles had no hesitation about declaring him subversive of art.

A new well-trained generation of critics has been on the *qui vive* against any American playwright's effort to deal weightily with a serious subject. Throughout the decade playwrights have been criticized for any symptoms showing efforts to live above their intellectual or artistic incomes. A writer could expect no mercy from the vigilant few, whether he was Arthur Miller aiming at social drama with *Death of a Salesman* and *The Crucible*, or Archibald MacLeish training his sights on metaphysical poetic drama with *J.B.* To be serious without at least a good helping of irony has been enough to invite the charge of being solemn rather than serious, intellectual rather than intelligent.

[4] From *Theatre at the Crossroads* by John Gassner. Copyright © 1960 by Mollie Gassner. Reprinted by permission of Holt, Rinehart and Winston, Inc. New York. '60. p 127-9, 107-9. Mr. Gassner is a professor of drama at Yale University.

Awkwardness now is considered the great sin. Its presence is acceptable only when the author is a European writer (say, Claudel or Dostoevski) or when the American author belonged to an earlier aristocracy of letters (Henry James, for instance) and specialized in sensibility and manners. The heavyweight champion of the American stage, O'Neill, was considered finished at the beginning of the fifties. But he arose from the grave in 1956 and with José Quintero's successful off-Broadway revival of *The Iceman Cometh* and the Brodway success of his posthumously produced plays, *Long Day's Journey into Night* and *A Touch of the Poet,* he recovered and strengthened his position in the American theatre. Yet these successes have not altered the impression current in literary circles that our drama must move toward a new dispensation of intellectual refinement and artistic subtlety or else doom itself to failure. This impression prevails as the sixties open with no new prospects or promises.

Ten years ago pessimists could have concluded that the decline of purpose and passion everywhere else fated the theatre to experience the same softening. These fatalists were forced to correct their horoscopes somewhat as the years brought in rapid succession such vigorous productions as *Cat on a Hot Tin Roof* and *The Crucible.* But in 1950 the pessimists had enough evidence to support their suspicion that entropy had set in. The most telling evidence was not so much the failure of obviously worthless plays as the attentuation of plays possessing various degrees of merit; these works were prevented from attaining their maximum potential by some diffusion of interest or some contraction of vision or will. At least five such plays appeared on Broadway between 1950 and 1951: Odets' *The Country Girl;* Lillian Hellman's *The Autumn Garden;* Philip Barry's posthumous comedy, *Second Threshold,* as completed by Robert Sherwood; the poetic dramatization of Melville's *Billy Budd* by Louis O. Coxe and Robert Chapman; and Sidney Kingsley's dramatization of Arthur Koestler's remarkable novel, *Darkness at Noon.*

Signs of enervation have continued to appear ever since, as if a law of entropy were operative in a period of uncertainty and disillusionment. In 1958-1959 . . . the Pulitzer Prize poetic drama, *J.B.,* moved toward a tame conclusion, after hurling the challenge of Job against the miseries of the modern world. The appealing

Drama Critics Circle Award Play *A Raisin in the Sun* followed a conventional dramatic pattern, wavering between domestic comedy and drama of protest. Nevertheless, one simply cannot turn criticism into dismissal or indulge impatience or disappointment implacably without placing nearly all playwriting under a theatre-destroying interdict. One way to insure the continuation of entropy is to use it as a reason or excuse for summarily invalidating all the dramatic work of the period. Another way is to refuse to recognize defect or insufficiency in any dramatic work that has earned respect. . . .

We are still suffering, both in production and playwriting, from a want of focus. The majority of playwrights have given slight thought to anything but the grinding out of plays. They have been too often content with *aperçus* and expedients. I doubt that any artist sees his problems from every angle or fully understands the infinitely complex essence of his creativity. Even such singularly lucid playwrights as Shaw and Bertolt Brecht have not always understood their creative processes or realized the possibilities or limitations of their procedures. Yet the effort to understand one's own aims must continue, and such effort must focus, as a small number of playwrights like Brecht and Arthur Miller realized, on the whole character and point of modern playwriting. Neither critic nor playwright can afford to operate solely by instinct in our confounding and dismaying age. After having participated in some seventy-five stage productions and struggling with a great many more (between nine and ten thousand!) unproduced play-scripts I have become convinced that the mindless and passionless flux in our theatre is egregiously wasteful, even if I don't know how to correct this condition.

In the early forties there was common ground in the aggravation of crisis, the preservation of freedom, and the simple problem of national survival. But little of this got itself translated into effective dramatic art. We experienced brief release from dramaturgic controls and collective anxiety through the pure-in-heart, trust-in-the-little-people plays of William Saroyan, beginning with *My Heart's in the Highlands*. We tried, rather unsuccessfully, to respond to the war's call for heroic drama. It is true that Sidney Kingsley's *The Patriots*, a lesson in national unity, treated Hamilton and Jefferson with appreciative intelligence. But a program of historical drama was successfully initiated in

America only in outdoor pageant theatre, chiefly in the South under the inspired leadership of Paul Green, who started it with *The Lost Colony* several years before World War II.

The outstanding Broadway play of this period of crisis was undoubtedly *The Skin of Our Teeth.* But Thornton Wilder's chronicle of man's precarious survival since the Ice Age and the Deluge, with its wonderful *Finnegans Wake* kind of synthesis of time past and time present, won little support in New York after it succeeded in confusing its tryout audiences.

After World War II we had a brief flurry of liberal problem plays. But no special kind of theatre arose in the early postwar years. A transformation of our theatre was not apparent even when the new playwrights—Williams, Miller, and Inge—started emerging after 1945. It was characteristic of the times that Williams in the fifties moved ahead with a free-wheeling eclecticism to become the new period's most thriving playwright. . . .

In the postwar period, we have returned to the habitual haphazardness of our theatre. The New York City Center, under the courageous guidance of indefatigable Jean Dalrymple, bravely continues its short theatrical seasons, but is dependent upon improvisation and expediency. The Phoenix Theatre, situated between Broadway and off-Broadway, has made costly efforts to present meaningful productions. But the management of Norris Houghton and T. E. Hambleton has been under constant economic pressure to resort to expedients and modify policy. The Phoenix was not given an opportunity in the fifties to organize its own company and create a repertory of classics and recent works of merit and significance. Dreams of establishing repertory theatres and creating a National Theatre failed to materialize despite the labors of many admirable persons at ANTA [American National Theatre and Academy], especially Robert Breen and Robert Whitehead.

A new college-trained generation of the fifties has taken an exalted view of tradition and a dim one of the loose ideal, self-expression. But its ablest representatives are interested primarily in close criticism, symbolist interpretation, lyric poetry, and literary drama. This generation has been understandably repelled by our disorderly theatre, scornful of its playwrights, and disdainful even of O'Neill. Very little, however, has occurred in the American theatre to alter its character as a haphazard enterprise.

Even off-Broadway production has operated in a generally opportunistic manner.

The anarchy of show business, the lack of a national theatre, and the generally inchoate condition of American cultural life makes exalted demands upon the professional stage quixotic. To hanker for unity or a unified sensibility, society, and culture can lead to nothing but withdrawal from the theatre as a vulgar occupation. It is apparent, at the beginning of the precarious decade of the sixties, that this anarchy is bound to continue. Neither a new art theatre reminiscent of the twenties nor a new theatre of social consciousness recalling the thirties has sent out any tap roots during the fifteen-year post-World-War-II period. We have encountered only the isolated careers of several talented new writers. Few theatrical developments of international import have come to our attention from other countries in the fifties, although Anouilh, Beckett, Ionesco, and Duerrenmatt have impressed us with individual plays. The important thing at this juncture is the persistence of individual effort and the incandescence of some particular play or production. Such liveliness of spirit and intelligence restores confidence in the theatre just when all confidence seems to have vanished.

SHOW BUSINESS IS ALL BUSINESS [5]

On the face of it, it would almost seem that the Broadway theatre has never been in better health, economically at least. With the number of new plays arriving each year pretty well stabilized over the past decade at about seventy (compared with 260 thirty years ago), and with the number of theatres holding at thirty-two (against eighty only twenty years ago), box office receipts and audiences have been mounting. During the 1958-1959 season, in fact, 11,720,000 theatre-goers paid more than $40,150,000 to see seventy-one Broadway dramas, comedies and musicals—an audience increase of 863,000 and a box office boost of $3,000,000 over the 1957-1958 season. What's more, for the first time in the history of the theatre, last year saw weeks in which more than $1,000,000 passed into the till—and not one such week, but eight.

This is the outward face of prosperity; behind it lies the inner face of trouble. For, despite the record audiences and gross,

[5] From article by Richard Hammer, journalist. *The Nation.* 189:172-3. S. 26, '59. Reprinted by permission.

the season as a whole ended up $500,000 in the red. And, as usual, five out of every six shows were financial flops (the percentage of artistic failures was even higher). Costs of everything continued, and still continue, to mount. To bring a straight drama to a Broadway house now involves an outlay of $100,000 or more (three times as much as twenty years ago, twice as much as ten years ago), while the cost of producing a musical may run to the astronomical total of $350,000 to $400,000. Merely to keep pace with operating expenses, without doing anything at all toward paying off the original investment, a straight play must gross $20,000 or more every week at the box office. This means, in terms of audiences, 60 per cent to 70 per cent of capacity at every performance, with the entire orchestra floor sold. The needs of a musical are even greater. Little wonder, then, that only smash hits last for more than a few weeks and that few producers take a chance on anything new or with a potentially limited audience.

In some cases, certainly, there are legitimate reasons for increased costs: the salaries of supporting and minor actors have at last reached a livable level, as have those of backstage personnel. The costs of materials—scenery, lighting, costumes, advertising and the like—have gone up not only in the theatre, but all over. But where some cost rises have been inevitable, and even desirable, others are in a different category. Theatre owners, with several plays competing for each of their houses, now demand a larger share of the receipts, higher guarantees against losses, and sometimes even reductions in their share of such expenses as stagehands, advertising and the like. The stagehands' unions, watching the decline in the number of playhouses and the resultant contraction in available jobs, have demanded, and gotten, regulations establishing a minimum number of jobs for each theatre and carefully limiting the functions of each worker. And because these are strictly minimum regulations, a show which has a higher budget or a larger cast is required to hire more stagehands—even if the additional men have nothing to do but sit backstage and play poker.

Designers, lighting men, costumers and other technically creative people, working toward what they call "perfection," demand the best possible materials, regardless of budgets. The experience of one producer in this respect is particularly illuminating. Just before starting work on a new play, he had spent the summer watching a Connecticut neighbor build a new home at a cost of $25,000. At the theatre, that fall, his set designer asked for $40,000 to put up an impressionistic frame house on the stage. "Would it be cheaper," the producer finally asked in desperation, "if we installed real plumbing?"

As long as everyone else is getting theirs, the stars and the playwrights are not to be denied. Top stars can now command a base salary of $2,000 or more a week against a percentage of the gross. In some cases, this brings their weekly income to $7,000 or more—a high price to pay for talent on any terms. And the authors, long the forsaken men, have at last come into their own, largely through the intervention of their agents. Not only do authors draw their legitimately handsome royalties, but they now have gained a veto right over stars, cast, directors and other aspects of the production. While not too important to the authors themselves, this power gives the big agents a hold which is clearly apparent.

The man on the spot, then, is the man trying to put on the show: the producer. While meeting the demands of stars, the theatre owner and the unions, he must also try to protect his investment and that of his angels (still relatively easy to find). The easiest way for him to meet these financial pressures is to increase the price of tickets and deal with people who will buy them in huge lots. Thus, musicals . . . have a top of $9.90, while seats for straight plays . . . cost up to $7.50. At these rates, almost everyone except the expense-account boys and the theatre parties is priced right out of the audience.

That ubiquitous institution, the theatre party, has come to the rescue of many a producer in the last couple of years. With its aid, he can come into New York with an advance sale of $500,000 to $1 million or more, knowing that he's going to run for a good, long time and very probably turn a profit—or, at least, break even.

Arrangements for the theatre parties—there are thousands every year and the number is growing—are handled by any one of twelve different theatre-party agents, who get 6½ per cent of the price of each ticket. In some ways, these parties make it easier for a producer; in others, more difficult. If the producer has something the agents think will sell, then he's all set; they will work to get as many organizations as possible interested, and sell as many tickets as they can. But if the agents think the producer has a lemon, or a show which won't interest their clients, they will sit on their hands. (The tickets they handle, of course, go to organizations which in turn sell them at high premiums, which are tax deductible. Thus, the audience brought in by the agents don't generally go to the theatre because it is the theatre: they go because the $25 or $50 they pay over the ticket price make it a tax-deductible evening.)

The power of the party agents is obvious. With their control over vast audiences, they can break or make a show by their recommendation or lack of it. . . . [At one point] theatres were forced to call off a plan to experiment with an early, 7:30 P.M., curtain on Wednesday nights because agents had already booked 120-odd parties for these midweek nights.

Under all of these pressures—mounting costs which mean higher ticket prices which mean reliance on theatre parties and expense-account crowds—the New York theatre, at least on Broadway (and increasingly off Broadway, too), is losing its real audience. A love for the theatre is something that is built early in life and lasts a lifetime. But today, the newly-married young people, the kids out of college, just cannot afford to go. This potential audience doesn't exist any more; and the steady, every-week theatregoer has become a thing of the past.

With producers reluctant to take a chance on anything but pure entertainment, the vitality that was once New York theatre is gone. The effect is sometimes as baleful upon the critics as upon the theatre. Nowadays when an occasional producer does show a spark of vitality by putting on something even a little off-beat, critics are inclined to praise him. In their desperate attempt to save the theatre for the theatre, the critics, too, along with everyone else seem to have lost their critical judgment. Seriousness alone is not enough for a play; there must be artistic merit as well. The theatre isn't going to be saved by praising its every valiant failure.

What becomes obvious about the Broadway theatrical scene is that art and economics have become one and indissoluble. In order to try to make money, the producers produce only what they think the majority want. Even the serious drama is generally only pseudoserious, but since it is "different," it is greeted with praise, may make some money (which Shakespeare rarely

does), and presents a general impression that things are returning to greatness. But the impression is only fleeting. The total
impression of the theatre in the United States today is of gloss
and polish and technical finesse; of an art form without art;
of a vital aspect of life without vitality.

OFF-BROADWAY THEATRE [6]

It is hard to classify today's off-Broadway theatre. The editors
of *Theatre Arts* magazine, for example, put everything not glori-
ously commercial, including colleges and universities in the Mid-
west, church groups in the Virgin Islands or Alaska, little theatres
in Dallas or Saginaw, into the off-Broadway category. Such
classification muddles the word "off-Broadway," for New York
City itself has at any given time perhaps three or four hundred
groups and theatres in active production. The term "off-Broadway" in any really definitive sense applies only to those New
York *professional* groups actively engaged in theatrical production
in places exclusive of theatres in the Times Square area. At the
height of the theatre season, in the winter, these groups, thus defined, number anywhere from thirty to fifty. It is partly the success of their predecessors of thirty to forty years ago which sparks
the creative drive of workers in the current off-Broadway theatre of such recent off-Broadway talents as Ben Gazzara, Ger-
aldine Page, José Quintero, Carmen Capalbo, Albert Salmi, William and Jean Eckert, and Jason Robards, Jr.; and it is partly
an irresistible urge to work in and contribute to the dramatic art
which causes off-Broadway to burgeon and to produce so pro-
lifically.

The real post-World-War-II renaissance of off-Broadway
theatre started in 1950 when a group of intrepid young actors met
in a loft in Greenwich Village and decided to pool their money
and talent under the designation of The Loft Players. They spent
that summer operating a stock company in Woodstock, New York,
and upon returning to New York City took a ten-year lease on
the defunct Greenwich Village Inn at 5 Sheridan Square. Because of zoning regulations the theatre was forced to operate

[6] From the Introduction to *The Off-Broadway Theatre: Seven Plays,* edited by
Richard A. Cordell and Lowell Matson. © Copyright 1959 by Random House, Inc.
Reprinted by permission. p xvi-xxi. Mr. Cordell is an author and professor of English
at Purdue University.

under a cabaret license. Money shortage and licensing difficulties delayed the opening of their first production until February, 1951. It was a revival of a moderate Broadway success, *Dark of the Moon* by Howard Richardson and William Berney, and garnered four off-Broadway awards for the newly formed organization, now called Circle in the Square.

The theatre still resembles a night club with horseshoe seating, a ring of small tables and a snack bar in the lounge. It seats 270 people and has a small art gallery with changing shows. To supplement box office income, Circle in the Square has sponsored on "dark" nights jazz concerts, poetry recitals, children's theatre, and concerts.

As originally constituted, Circle in the Square included some twenty-two actors, alternating between small and lead roles and interested in producing unusual plays, whether formerly produced on Broadway or not, for runs not to exceed two months; however, some of their successes have had New York record runs because of popular demand. They have specialized in turning Broadway failures into successes, among them Giraudoux's *The Enchanted,* Steinbeck's *Burning Bright,* Williams' *Summer and Smoke,* Capote's *The Grass Harp,* O'Neill's *The Iceman Cometh,* and Mayer's *Children of Darkness.* Other productions have been Benavente's *Bonds of Interest,* Lorca's *Yerma,* Hayes's *Girl on the Via Flaminia,* Sierra's *Cradle Song,* and Schnitzler's *La Ronde.*

The Circle in the Square production of *Summer and Smoke* in the season of 1952-1953 ran for 357 performances, and is credited by some observers as having by itself sparked the off-Broadway revival. Its production of *The Iceman Cometh* ran for 565 performances, the longest run in history of a play by O'Neill. Out of sixteen productions at the theatre, José Quintero, a charter member of the group, a theatre novice who was a graduate from the University of Southern California with some training at the Goodman Theatre, has directed all but two. Quintero's brilliant handling of the arena style of production, in contrast to the inept productions of an earlier arena group at the Edison Hotel, has assured the success of the theatre. Joining with his coproducers, Ted Mann and Leigh Connell, Quintero in 1957 produced and directed the award-winning *Long Day's Journey Into Night* on Broadway.

In 1952 William de Lys, a promoter fascinated by the theatre, took a seven-year lease on the old Hudson Playhouse at 121 Christopher Street. At an estimated cost of $143,000 he refurbished and glorified the dilapidated house with the intent of establishing a club theatre, and of selling subscriptions for thirty-day runs of productions before sending them out on tour in the East. An opening season of nine productions was planned. The theatre was cut down in seating capacity from 600 to 299 in order to meet Equity's specification as a "little theatre," and modern lighting, sound and other equipment was installed. A stage thirty feet wide and thirty-four feet deep, comparable in size to that of the average Broadway house, was built. The Theatre de Lys opened with a production of an inferior musical entitled *Frankie and Johnny,* which met a scathing critical reception and closed the next day. The theatre went into receivership and thereafter experienced a procession of productions, including *End as a Man* and *Bullfight,* which booked into the house through a holding company. In the summer of 1953 the theatre housed a repertory company. Finally in 1954 Stanley Chase and Carmen Capalbo, a graduate of the Yale Drama School, opened their production of the Brecht-Blitzstein-Weill *Threepenny Opera.* In 1955 the theatre was sold to Lucille Lortel and Chase and Capalbo became its managers and coproducers. *Threepenny Opera* . . . played to capacity houses . . . , employing in its history over two hundred artists, and establishing an off-Broadway long-run record. Theatre de Lys, still bearing the name of its original founder, is one of the best equipped and most delightful of the off-Broadway theatres.

Off-Broadway theatres come in all shapes and forms. At the eastern edge of Greenwich Village on East Fourth Street are two playhouses which have achieved a reputation as the home of modern classics. The first is the Downtown Theatre at 85 East Fourth Street in what was, before the establishment of the theatre in 1956, a Ukrainian Club; it still maintains on the second floor a convenient bar for club members and patrons. The house seats 150 and has a deep platform stage at the end of the auditorium. It was established by William and Elizabeth Landis, graduates in drama respectively from the University of Washington and the University of Iowa. The Downtown Theatre since its inception has rapidly become the New York home of Shaw, having produced *Arms and the Man, Man of Destiny, Candida, The Philanderer, You Never Can Tell,* and the American première of *In Good King Charles's Golden Days,* which opened in January, 1957, and ran for over a year.

Immediately next door to the Downtown Theatre, at 83 East Fourth Street, is the Fourth Street Playhouse. David Ross, a young graduate of the University of Minnesota, renovated the building, once a synagogue, later a supper club, and after that the home of two now defunct playhouses—the Royal Playhouse and Two by Four Productions—into an arena theatre seating 175. Ross says: "I have nothing against new plays, which are the lifeblood of our theatre. Fortunately there always seems to be a showcase for deserving new playwrights. Meanwhile, the classics are being neglected." With that philosophy he instituted a season of Chekhov in 1956 including new translations of *The Sea Gull, Uncle Vanya,* and *The Cherry Orchard; The Dybbuk* was also revived. With rare persuasiveness, and the financial backing to make it possible, Ross has been able to acquire such distinguished actors as Morris Carnovsky, Franchot Tone, Signe Hasso, and Clarence Derwent for his productions. The Fourth Street Playhouse can rightly be called the American home of Chekhov. [In 1962 Ross moved uptown, but retained his off-Broadway status with a small theatre in the west fifties.—Ed.]

Another estimable source of off-Broadway productions is the Greenwich Mews Theatre in the basement of the Brotherhood Church on West Thirteenth Street. Sponsored jointly by the Village Presbyterian Church and the Brotherhood Synagogue, it was founded in 1950 with one hundred writer-director-actor members as an interfaith, interracial theatre specializing in new plays with social themes. The theatre has been run on a voluntary contribution basis and has presented such plays as the widely hailed *Me, Candido* and Loften Mitchell's all-Negro *A Land Beyond the River.* Recently the theatre gave the American première of a new adaption of Gorki's *The Courageous One.* In March 1958, Greenwich Mews Theatre signed an agreement with a retail workers' union, District 65, Retail, Wholesale and Department Store Union, by means of which the union gives the playhouse financial support in return for conducting a workshop for union members.

The Provincetown Playhouse still operates on MacDougal Street, booking in productions of indpendent off-Broadway producers. The Rooftop Theatre, reached by taking an elevator to the fifth floor at 111 East Houston Street, was once a burlesque house, and recently presented a smoothly professional première of *Clérambard* by Marcel Aymé, with Claude Dauphin, and Joyce's *Ulysses in Nighttown*. The Renata Theatre at 144 Bleecker Street was once a supper club and has been redecorated and refurbished into one of the most comfortable playhouses off Broadway. The Martinique Theatre at Broadway and Thirty-second Street and the Barbizon Plaza Theatre at 106 Central Park South take their names from the hotels which house them. The small but elegant Theatre Marquee, at 110 East Fifty-ninth Street, was originally Isadora Duncan's dance studio. The Gate Theatre and the Cricket Theatre, both at 162 Second Avenue, were, respectively, a Baptist church and the church gymnasium. The Cherry Lane Theatre at 38 Commerce Street was remodeled from a box factory in 1924 by Edna St. Vincent Millay, Marie St. Gaudens, and Cleon Throckmorton into a showcase for experimental productions. It has had a long succession of producers in its continuous thirty-five-year history, including John Dos Passos and John Howard Lawson for the New Playwrights Theatre in 1927-1928. Their third production that season was *The International* by Lawson with a distinguished cast including Franchot Tone and George Tobias. Recent productions of Sean O'Casey's *The Plough and the Stars,* Paul Vincent Carroll's *The Wise Have Not Spoken,* Samuel Beckett's *Endgame,* and the American première and record run of O'Casey's *Purple Dust,* tend to label the Cherry Lane Theatre as the American home of Irish dramatists.

The Phoenix Theatre at Second Avenue and East Twelfth Street is, perhaps, the most impressive of the off-Broadway projects. Originally designed and built for the great Yiddish actor Maurice Schwartz in 1927, it seats 1,186. During the depression the theatre lost almost a million dollars and in 1934 became a motion picture house. In 1953 it was taken over by T. Edward Hambleton and Norris Houghton with the intention of establishing an art theatre and a repertory house patterned after London's Lyric Hammersmith Theatre. They renamed the former Yiddish Art Theatre the Phoenix, symbolic of the new rising out of the ashes of the old. Professional actors and workers in show business backed the initial venture with an original capitalization of $125,000. Its first production in 1953 was *Madam, Will You Walk?* by Sidney Howard. The Phoenix has presented about sixty productions—half of which have been classics—utilizing almost seven hundred artists and musicians, and playing to an aggregate of a million people. With its production in 1954 of *The Golden Apple,* the John Latouche-Jerome Moross musical, the Phoenix hit its stride. Since then it has produced such classics as Cocteau's *The Infernal Machine,* Schiller's *Mary Stuart,* Shakespeare's *Coriolanus,* and Shaw's *Saint Joan,* employing the leading acting and production talents of America and England. The theatre has housed many foreign visitors such as the French Canadian Players, the Stratford (Ontario) Company, and the French mimist, Marcel Marceau. . . . The Phoenix has rapidly become the leading art theatre in America, attracting such an intellectual, literate audience that wags have called it an "egghead operation." [In 1961 the Phoenix moved uptown to a new home, a much smaller theatre on East 74th Street.—Ed.]

The policy of the Phoenix is to plan for a four-week run in a continuous, stable producing situation in order to release actors, directors, playwrights, and designers from the pressures forced on them by the hit-or-flop pattern of Broadway, a pattern that too often has limited their freedom to create. Hambleton has stated:

"Our project is not like the usual off-Broadway theatre. We are not a showcase for new, young talent. That is important, of course, and we want to see youngsters get a break. But what we are providing is a place where stars and professional actors can act without the hit psychology lurking in the background.". . .

Off-Broadway theatre in the late fifties of the twentieth century is still insurgent, as it was in the teens and twenties of the century. But it has a different basic complexion. The theatre of Provincetown and of Washington Square sprang from literary frustrations, from a determination to provide an outlet for an important new American drama. It is perhaps regrettable that off-Broadway theatre today is more concerned than it was in the early years in providing a showcase for acting and directing talents with the hope that Broadway, or Hollywood, will become interested. It is true, however, that most of the plays given are of a nature which Broadway either has rejected, produced without commercial success, or else totally ignored. . . .

THEATRE ACROSS THE COUNTRY [7]

It is not easy to speak of the professional theatre outside New York, for the simple reason that, although there is very little of it, there is also very little interchange of information about what is happening in the different states of the Union. Those few cities that maintain professional resident theatres tend to feel self-sufficient, engrossed in their own problems. It is equally hard to make any generalizations about the community theatres, for exactly the opposite reason: there are thousands of them, and no single individual can hope to sort out the good and the bad in so widespread an activity. Add the academic theatres, the summer- and the winter-stock theatres, and it is clear that there is an extraordinarily wide range of theatrical activity throughout the country.

For the past few months I have been traveling about, looking at, among other things, the theatrical situation, and especially the professional theatre. What I found everywhere was refreshing enthusiasm, but a certain lack of reflection about what exactly a regional theatre can and cannot do.

It cannot, for instance, enter into competition with Broadway, though it can very usefully enlarge and supplement the kind of work done off Broadway by increasing the number of professional theatres outside New York. And it is here that more could be done. Though it is true that a large proportion of the actors, playwrights and directors on Broadway started their careers in either community or university theatre, the professional theatre outside New York barely exists, and it could do nothing but good to an overcrowded calling if that theatre were strengthened—not so much in quality (which is high) but in number.

Regional theatre in the United States has suffered from the fact that so heavy a concentration of talent is caught fast in New York life. In Washington, Chicago, San Francisco and Houston, however, an effort has been made to persuade career actors to accept out-of-town assignments, and on the whole it has been successful. Admittedly, if a theatre is in a position to pay its actors a proper living wage, it is likely, sooner or later, to jeopardize the situation of any other theatre in the area; and since it is

[7] From article by Alan Pryce-Jones, author and journalist, formerly editor of the *Times Literary Supplement* (London). *Theatre Arts.* 45:25-6+. My. '61. Reprinted by permission of *Theatre Arts* Magazine.

easier for an established professional theatre—like Mrs. Nina Vance's Alley Theatre in Houston—to raise outside financial help, those local theatres that depend for their existence on private support may feel that they are being driven out of business. But the half-dozen or so resident professional theatres in the country are obviously not sufficiently important numerically to disturb the balance of an enterprise that is mainly in the hands of community theatre; and at least it has been shown that New York actors are willing to work elsewhere if the inducement is good enough.

If I compare the regional theatres of the United States and England, I find significant differences. In England, the influence of London on provincial theatre is much more sharply marked than that of New York on the other states of the Republic. That is largely because no city in the British Isles is physically very far from London, and so there is less reason to decentralize the arts than in a country cut to continental scale. There are, however, a number of repertory theatres with professional companies throughout the English country towns, and several of these have made a practice of commissioning, or first presenting, new plays of quality. For instance, Coventry put on the trilogy of Arnold Wesker, of which *Roots* lately reached New York; and a far smaller city, Salisbury, gave an excellent account of a promising play by Doris Lessing—better known as a novelist—that is unlikely ever to reach London. Similar enterprises exist all over the country—and I regret that they are not more frequent in the United States, in spite of the example set by Margo Jones in Dallas, when she initiated such international successes as *Inherit the Wind.*

Margo Jones is dead, and it is true that a new play was in rehearsal in Dallas while I was there; but notwithstanding all the drive and enterprise that exists throughout this country, there is no one with quite the theatrical flair of Joan Littlewood, who has made a point of settling her small theatre into the heart of a London East End borough. She tries to use local talent, to find local plays, to attract a local audience, and she has largely succeeded in making the Theatre Royal a kind of microcosm of the real-life existence—poverty-stricken, hard-working, unpretentious—that surrounds it. Might not a city like San Francisco do the same?

Not that San Francisco lags behind. The Actor's Workshop activities of Jules Irving and Herbert Blau are among the best things in the American theatre. But I can picture what might be done with the unique opportunities of the city if they could be canalized directly into the theatre, after the fashion of the Stratford Theatre Royal. It may be asking too much to expect a Brecht to turn up in order to hold a mirror to the life of our own times; yet if the regional theatre is to use its full potentiality, some such miracle can be expected. A city like New York is too vast and too varied to be captured on the stage. But there is plenty of scope for making new theatre out of the more compact atmosphere of the great regional centers. Furthermore, it is possible to adapt such plays to a tight budget—and regional theatres are never flush. . . .

No theatre will flourish unless it attracts the right kind of director. A very great deal of hard work is necessary in order to conjure up the right working conditions and the right atmosphere. The examples of Mrs. Zelda Fichandler at Arena Stage in Washington, D.C., of John Reich at the Goodman Memorial Theatre, Chicago, and Paul Baker in Dallas, show what can be done to bring a professional air to what might otherwise have been a theatre of good intentions only. So many handicaps have to be overcome. Arena Stage, for instance, has had to function in a building both too small and too obviously not designed as a theatre. Money has now been raised, and plans drawn, for a fine new building. But in order to get thus far, the managing director has had to put in an immense amount of personal effort in addition to organizing current productions. Again, in Dallas, the new theatre designed by Frank Lloyd Wright may possess an exciting elevation; from the audience's point of view it may be extremely comfortable—I know no auditorium with a better wide-angled view of the stage from all parts of the house; but as a theatre to work in, it leaves much to be desired. Backstage, space is cramped, and there is an exit ramp so steep that it almost qualifies as a chute. True, Wright was not experienced in building theatres until this opportunity was given him at the end of his life; but it is regrettable that he set so much emphasis on the dramatic impact of his design and so little on its practicality.

Public-spirited individuals everywhere do a great work in financing the theatre, and it is clearly right that such local support should both be sought and given. But if the professional theatre is to flourish it is equally clear that outside help must be forthcoming. And in that regard the British system may be worth noting. For in England it is not to individuals that the theatre outside London mainly looks, but to the local authorities, who are empowered to levy a small tax in order to raise funds for the arts, while in the background there stands the government-backed Arts Council, which may help still further in exceptional circumstances. This impersonal method of bringing money to the theatre avoids the temptation of sacrificing too much to the presence of a star or stars—as at Stratford, Connecticut—who will bring the public to a series of festival performances without enough regard to the over-all quality of the productions.

There are also the academic theatres to be considered, and here it appears that a good deal is to be desired. Possibly the most beautiful modern theatre of medium size in the United States is the new Loeb Memorial Theatre in Cambridge, Massachusetts. It is also one of the best-equipped; each unit in the complicated process of creating a play—from scene painting to rehearsal, from storage space to switchboard, from the multiple machinery of a modern stage to the comfort of the actors—has been accorded equal, minute attention. But having built the theatre, the Harvard authorities have discovered no important use for it. I dare not risk generalizing about a subject that involves close knowledge not only of theatre conditions but of university curriculums and their workings, but I formed an impression that those great institutions in the East best able, in theory, to do good work, had achieved less than their rivals in Kansas, Ohio or Iowa, say, which have contrived to maintain a higher standard of interest and skill in teaching the art of the theatre.

Any discussion of the regional theatre inevitably boils down to two main questions. The first is money. The community theatres have worked out their own system of finance, depending on the good will and active help of small individual groups. But I suggest that the potentialities of the theatre will best be fulfilled when more of the weight is shifted from individuals to the community as a whole. Some cities like Kansas City, Missouri, and Cincinnati have led the way in that respect, but too often help depends on the public spirit of the few. Such a condition is not only defeating to good theatre; it is also the antithesis of good economics, since it precludes any sort of long-term plan.

Then there is the question of casting. At present, regional professional theatres exist as so many separate entities, the directors of which only by chance get to hear of young actors who might be of service to them. Much closer cooperation will be needed in order to make the best use of available professional talent. It is impossible to break the hegemony of Broadway and off-Broadway. They must always serve as the center of dramatic life in this country. But the regional theatre is very much more than a nursery for the New York stage. It has needs of its own to fulfill. Those needs must be related more closely to the supply of money and talent available. In other words, the regional theatres—and especially the professional ones—must get to know one another better, so that not only individual cities but the whole country may get the theatre it deserves.

EUTERPE AND THE SOUND OF MUZAK [8]

Social critics earlier than De Tocqueville and more recent than Ortega y Gasset have concerned themselves with the place of the arts in a democracy and, being a notoriously self-conscious people, Americans have taken them seriously. In the field of concert music in particular those who would like to help the cause of the art have been far too willing to take the warnings of such experts at face value, without careful examination of the peculiarities of the situation. It is, to select an obvious analogy, as though economists attempted to account for the American economy in purely Marxist terms, without considering the limitations of Marx's formulation, the surprising flexibility of American governmental institutions or America's apparent social fluidity.

If we look at the matter closely, we can see that the problem which most worried Ortega y Gasset—that is, that newcomers to the arts would pollute tastes because they do not bring with them the proper values—is not really relevant in the concert hall. While it is true that in the nineteenth century popular taste in

[8] From "Some Observations on the Concert Audience" by Stuart Levine, assistant professor of English, University of Kansas, and editor of the *Midcontinent American Studies Journal.* 15:152-66. Summer '63. © *American Quarterly.* Reprinted by permission.

the United States to a considerable extent did corrupt concert music (and examination of any of the volumes of memoirs written by barnstorming virtuosi will bear this out), it is also true that we did not have at the time a concert audience large enough to be worthy of the name. Whether they knew it or not, the barnstormers were functioning as popular entertainers. And what is more, the situation in the twentieth century is totally different. If anything, composers have been hampered not by too much audience influence, but by too little.

The special problem of music (and this is an oversimplification) is that for the first time in the modern world the composer in the early part of this century got too far ahead of his audience. Composers have been shocking audiences for centuries, but the gap between audience and composer certainly was never so great as it was then. A sign of its magnitude is that in this century we have had the unusual phenomenon of major composers writing music with no specific performance, commission, prize competition or artist in mind. The composer, deprived of that immediate audience reaction which, whatever its disadvantages, is an essential part of any healthy art, retreated to his garret, from which generations of philanthropists, propagandists and musical reformers have attempted to rescue him. They will concern themselves with vigorous windmill-tilting and assaults on dead horses. They are worried, for instance, about listener comprehension of the new music; this is no longer a serious problem: decades of movie and television sound-tracks have conditioned us to accept, even to "understand," almost anything which the composer is likely to do.

It is revealing to compare what happened to the concert audience in the fifty years from 1900 to 1950 to what happened in jazz in the ten years beginning, let us say, with 1943. The situations are surprisingly similar. Some time during the Second World War, for reasons which are partially social and partially a matter of a logical development of their art, the front line of jazz performers lost touch with the audience. In a very brief time, these men reached a position so far ahead of what their listeners could comprehend that the music which they were producing seemed as mad to its listeners as did the music at those famous concerts early in the century which produced riots and flying vegetables. It took roughly ten years for an audience to catch up with what the bopsters had done, and, just as the various directions in which the concert musical rebellion at the turn of the century were woven together in a synthesis usually called the International Style, the developments in bop were assimilated into the fabric of what came to be known as Modern Jazz. Jazz reached a workable solution to its audience problem in ten years as compared to the fifty it took concert music. It has as yet been unable to solve the problem of patronage.

Concert composers are a little better off: the universities have taken over the job which the eighteenth century patron and the nineteenth century concert audience used to perform, so that by now the garret has been transformed, by and large, into a poor man's split-level in a faculty slum. Critic and crusader, however, go on undaunted, believing that all it takes to restore the composer to his rightful position (whatever that is supposed to be— no composer in the last two centuries, to my knowledge, has ever been able to support himself solely on the proceeds earned from music written for the concert hall, though a few have managed if they wrote music for the stage) is propaganda for the new music aimed at some hypothetical established body of listeners.

The facts are that the special reasons for the failure of the new music to hold a large audience are unrelated to this line of thinking. They are simple, almost physical, and they are peculiar —to this one art. I will list them briefly.

1. The new music, of whatever variety or quality, is music of great tension and demands careful listening. It will not work (as much of the good music of the past will) as fashionable background to a cocktail party. You can't even read to it. And since few people, even serious music lovers, really spend more than a few minutes a week listening intently, it does not get listened to in the home.

2. If it is any good, it works very well in the concert hall, even when performed for musically unsophisticated audiences. But concert managers are afraid of it. They believe that it frightens away audiences, and, what is worse, they know that it is terribly expensive to perform. The cost shows up less in royalties than in rehearsal time; if you study the programs of the major orchestras, you discover that the appearance of a new work

on a program usually means the appearance of a thundering herd of war horses in the programs surrounding its performance. New works take extra rehearsal time; rehearsal time is frightfully expensive; all orchestras are broke. So the new piece must be padded about with works from what orchestra librarians call "the first repertoire," works which can be played with little or no rehearsal.

Moreover, any work, new or old, takes repeated listening to establish itself; very few new works, even most of those which the critics take to on first hearing, are ever reperformed. The late Serge Koussevitzky had a deserved reputation as a "pioneer." Under him the Boston Symphony premiered an impressive number of new works. But if one reads back through the program books of the Symphony, one quickly discovers that most of the new works performed were played once or twice, then forgotten. . . .

3. And this is our main point today: it is my thesis that if we examine the listening career of the individual music lover, we find that a taste for the new music is usually the last taste he acquires, if he acquires it at all. I believe that the concert audience is pyramidical in structure, and that tastes are dynamic, not static. As one moves upwards from the base of the pyramid, where tastes are limited to the familiar chestnuts and the best-known music of the best-known composers, the ranks of the audience thin out. The new music, alas, occupies a position near the apex.

If these assertions are true—and I hope to demonstrate that they are—the way to get more listeners at the apex would be to enlarge the pyramid: before there can be more customers for the product which the avant-garde is selling, we must get more traffic in the store. How do people come to like concert music? How large is the audience?

Much of what little reliable data we have on this latter topic comes from a series of studies financed by the American Federation of Musicians in the years following the Second World War. While these data are limited in many ways and certainly out of date, they at least indicate unambiguously that the concert audience, however defined, is growing.

CASH OUTLAY FOR ADMISSIONS TO MOTION PICTURES COMPARED TO
THAT FOR CONCERTS, OPERAS AND LEGITIMATE THEATRE
(in millions of dollars)

Year	Movies	Index	Concerts, etc.	Index
1939	659	100	32	100
1940	709	107.6	36	112.5
1941	756	114.7	40	125.0
1942	924	140.2	48	150.0
1943	987	149.8	68	212.5
1944	1175	178.3	82	256.2
1945	1359	191.0	80	250.0
1946	1427	216.5	91	284.4
1947	1380	209.4	103	321.9

Limitations: (1) Since the figures are based on admissions receipts, records and radio are specifically excluded. (2) The "concert" figures include receipts for admissions to plays. (3) The figures stop at the beginning of a great boom in concert music triggered by the long-playing record and the high-fidelity craze. (4) The movies in 1947 provide a poor basis for comparison; they were just entering a brief period of declining receipts. Source: *International Musician*, December 1948.

How fast it is growing I do not know. It is discouraging to note that its size until about the period of the A. F. of M. study was a steady 1 per cent of the total population: it kept pace with population growth but seemed unable to engage a proportionally larger group. I am prone to trust those rather subjective indices, the mass media, which, in the years since the study, give one the distinct feeling that the rate of growth has finally increased; I think that something which one wants to label "common sense" tells us that increased leisure means increased audience, but of course one should be wary of common sense when dealing with social and cultural issues. For our purposes, it hardly matters anyway, since even were the audience merely keeping pace proportionally, it would still be growing. If it is growing, new listeners must be coming from somewhere. Where?

Here is another list: six hypothetical "paths" to the concert hall. First: undoubtedly many people inspire a taste for good music simply because it is present in the atmosphere of the homes in which they are brought up. If one reads the music critics, particularly the big ones in the eastern papers, and especially Virgil Thomson, one soon learns that most of them tacitly assume that all sophisticated listeners come from this source. That most people agree with them can be inferred from the aura of snobbism which surrounds the concert hall; the assumption is that "our kind of people" like good music; these critics are distinctly writing for "our kind of people." If you are not "in," you are "out," and your snickers only demonstrate how real you think the difference is. But the idea that this process, which we can call "the traditional path," is the only way to the concert hall is absurd, first, because it presupposes a more rigid class structure than we have; second, because, as we have seen, the concert audience is growing, and the hypothetical social class to which this group of critics thinks it is addressing itself is precisely that class which students of population and fertility tell us is unable to keep pace with rapid population growth. This explanation would make sense were our society clearly split between "mass" man and "elite" man. But, as we have seen Daniel Bell [noted sociologist] argue, it is not.

If we return to the *International Musician* and the A.F. of M., we can discern the outlines of a second path to the concert hall (and we should make clear from the outset that these paths overlap and intertwine). According to that magazine, as of 1948, one out of every eight Americans played a musical instrument, and the author of the article in which this figure was reported goes on to say that it is "axiomatic that the audiences for professional performances of all types, popular and serious, are recruited at least fifty per cent from amateurs who have taken a fling at playing an instrument." One would like to know where on earth the author came up with his figure, but his point is certainly well taken. Certainly amateurs pick up an interest in music from playing. But if we examine the type of music which they play, we discover some interesting facts: most amateurs who participate in instrumental playing belong to bands; almost all band music is what we will later define as standard music. Those who do not for the most part also play standard music—popular songs which have become "standards," light classics, old favorites, popularized versions of the more familiar classics. This is easy enough to document; one has merely to examine the selections included in elementary and intermediate music instruction books for the various instruments.

Then I suppose that one should map a third path, that taken by those attracted to music by the hi-fi craze. The totally naïve listener who buys a rig has to buy some records. Presumably he starts with pops—the hit parade—but if he wants to show off his device, he has to buy LP's. Since most LP's are not really pops— the hit parade comes out on 78's and 45's—and since he will soon tire of recordings of sonic boom and cannon, the chances are good that he too will turn to standard music. Perhaps this is as far as he will ever get: 101 Strings and no content. But he may get farther.

Yet a fourth path is that of the music appreciation industry (or "racket," as one hostile critic calls it) and music education; I group them together not to imply anything about their relative merits but for convenience and brevity. I have no idea of the ultimate effectiveness of compulsory music education—the so-called "appreciation" courses required in many school systems— beyond the subjective reports of friends and students who have gone through them. They say that generally such courses are ineffective except in the cases of students already highly motivated to learn about concert music.

Motivation, which would seem to be the critical element in the grade and high schools, certainly is the critical element on the college level. What is going on is perhaps best understood in terms of reference-group theory. (This is a useful sociological concept designed to enable one to pin down the sources of ideas, ideals, attitudes, value-judgments, etc., by discovering from which groups the subject has acquired them, against which groups, in other words, he is measuring himself. If one were studying a group of students, for example, one might expect to find among their important reference groups their peers, their parents, their teachers, members of professional or fraternal groups, and so forth—any group to which the subjects might "refer" themselves.) If we pick the brain of a hypothetical serious-minded student and attempt to discover what he wants to get out of college, I think that we will find that, besides specific or specialized train-ing, it is something which can be defined, albeit vaguely, as an understanding of matters which people he admires or would like to imitate care about. A recent exploratory study of reference groups on a large campus, besides demonstrating that it is almost impossible to pin down a subject's reference groups without the sort of prompting which gives the gag away and invalidates the study, did suggest something of the sort. If the people to whom the student in one manner or another "refers" himself are interested in good books, art and music, he feels that he should know enough about such matters to enjoy them himself and/or to be able to talk about them. Most of us are, I believe, aware of how common this attitude is, especially among our better students.

Presumably, if the student does not pick up the requisite information socially or through required courses, he will go out of his way to acquire it. He is thus *using* whatever course he takes to equip himself for what is probably best understood as a change in social class, although he himself, perhaps through double-think, does not refer to class. "Educated," "intelligent," "sensitive," "knowledgeable," "people who count": these are the ways the students describe those they wish to emulate; they do not use the term "upper class," probably because this would imply a lack of democratic feeling and an acknowledgment of their own inferior class position at the present. If classes in our society should be understood not merely in terms of cash income but also in terms of style of life (which includes tastes and interests) and if, as also seems obvious, the college is for a great many students a place in which to cast oneself in the mold of a desired level of society, it would not be surprising to find students using introductory art and music courses for social purposes. (I should make clear that I am neither applauding nor criticizing the process; I do not want to imply anything about the sincerity of the student's commitment to the arts.)

Moreover, motivation of this type would seem also to account for the prosperity of the do-it-yourself culture industry. The magazines are full of invitations to join clubs which offer a quick introduction to the better things in life; all such advertisements stress the "informative booklets by well-known authorities" which accompany each selection. The entire come-on is quite consciously designed to suggest that the club offers answers to the question which the novitiate wants answered: How can I learn about those things which people I want to be like talk about?

But I am convinced that by far the most worn path to the concert hall runs through that music most despised—and perhaps deservedly so—by critic and connoisseur, so-called "standard music." By this I mean such things as "all-time favorites," popularized versions of the classics, "popular classics," the sound of Muzak and other sonic wallpaper, Kostelanetz, Waring and even Liberace: in short, all that "middle-brow slush and slop" which music historians have found aesthetically less interesting than pops, rock 'n' roll, hillbilly and even rock-a-billy, and compared to which the Twist is an artistic movement of a great significance. . . .

It would seem, then, that the best plan for the crusaders for the new music to follow would be to "lay off" their favorite targets, standard music and the war horses, and to concentrate instead on helping nature take its course. It is easy enough to see practical ways in which this can be done. For example, when the Montovani orchestra (perhaps "organization" would be a better word) made its American tour a year or so ago, it would have been helpful had a few serious music critics in different cities attended and reported. They would not have had to lower their standards in any way. An honest description of what went on would have sufficed to make clear to those who attended the concert just what the music they were listening to represented, and even to suggest to them that the "real thing" might be preferable. Similarly, an understanding of the manner in which listeners get to the concert hall might give the programers of educational concerts clearer principles on which to select works. I have played hundreds of educational concerts, and can report that school children are bored by most of the stuff performed at them. But they respond well to what musicians call "real rousers"—melodic and emotional late romantic music, noisy overtures, contemporary works with strong rhythmic vitality, even if, as was sometimes the case, of questionable worth. Most of the audience for the new music is recruited from the existing concert audience. One should encourage anything which will enlarge its ranks.

As to the larger problem of the arts in a mass society, I would say that the development of the American musical scene has been so totally different from anything which an earlier student of democratic culture could have predicted that we had best base our generalizations on empirical grounds. Alexis de Tocqueville's fear of a prevailing mediocrity in the arts makes no sense for concert music precisely because it *does* make sense for popular music, and popular music simply did not exist in his time: undoubtedly popular tastes corrupt the quality of our popular music (although even that has its defenders . . .), but the entire process serves to protect the concert music from corruption of any sort. It may be that popular and standard music serve as an artistic chastity belt to preserve the purity of our elite arts from the advances of tastes which would despoil them. But I think it more accurate to say that the popular audience is quite separate from the "elite" audience, and that when a listener makes the slow transition, he accepts fully what goes on in the concert hall. He in no sense corrupts concert music by his presence. If anything, he is liable at first to be too willing to conform to accepted canons of behavior. We do know that people new to a class are the most concerned with propriety and the rules. Silas Lapham spends a whole chapter worrying about whether or not to wear those white gloves. Silas may be in the concert hall because he is a culture vulture; he may be impressed by radio announcers whose tones suggest that they are introducing music pressed on records of burnished gold; he may, in short, be coming to music for class reasons, and perhaps the chances are even good that he will never develop beyond his present state. But, to mix a few metaphors, he has ears, and may very well enlarge his tastes. Many of his fellows are at the base of our pyramid. We know at least this much about Cheops' pyramid: it was not built from the top down.

THE DANCE IN AMERICA [9]

It is a fact that more than half a million paid admissions were registered by dance box offices in New York from September 1, 1961, to May 31, 1962. Just how many more it is not possible to say, but the figure given here would surely be increased by several thousand if a complete tabulation could be made.

The count of 511,209 covers the paid admission of the New York City Ballet, the American Ballet Theatre, Ballets U.S.A., the Martha Graham Company, the Leningrad Kirov Ballet, and

[9] From "The Big Count: Half a Million People Engaged in Non-Utilitarian Dance-Watching," article by Allen Hughes, dance critic, New York *Times*. New York *Times*. Sec. II, p 4X. Je. 10, '62. © 1962 by The New York Times Company. Reprinted by permission.

the Mazowsze (Polish) and Ukrainian folk dance companies. It includes also the dance performances given at Kaufmann Auditorium, the Henry Street Playhouse and the Brooklyn Academy of Music.

The given total does not cover the paid-admission figures for dance performances given at Hunter College Playhouse, the Fashion Institute of Technology, the Young Women's Christian Association Clark Center, Carnegie Hall, the Educational Alliance and Brooklyn College. Undoubtedly still other dance performances were given in New York that have not been included. . . .

We see, then, that the dance business in New York falls easily into the million-dollar-business category, a proof of popular support that everybody understands.

All these figures would probably have been still larger had there not been a pile-up of ballet companies competing with one another at the beginning of the season.

One week after the New York City Ballet opened its fall season, the Kirov Ballet made its American debut at the Metropolitan Opera House. Then, before the Kirov had left town, the American Ballet Theatre came in for two weeks at the 54th Street Theatre. While the Soviet company and Ballet Theatre were still playing, Ballets U.S.A. showed up at the ANTA Theatre.

It was too much of a good thing at one time, and each company suffered somewhat even while the public was outdoing itself and very likely setting concentrated ballet attendance records for New York.

Why so many people should pay so much money for something as non-utilitarian as dance-watching it is impossible to say. One can conclude only that they like it, and that does not explain anything. One cannot explain either why so many more are liking it now than used to. But they are.

Before World War II, dance was almost a dirty word for most Americans. A small, fiercely loyal band of devotees supported the dance activity of the time, but the rank and file suspected that members of the band were neither quite right nor quite bright. The rank-and-filer who entertained a notion that there might really be something of value in the dance was careful not to broadcast the fact too freely for fear of falling under suspicion himself.

The prejudices of those days seem to have passed for the most part. One can finally admit a liking for ballet without risking social ostracism, and the figures prove that one can go to see it without feeling like a member of a minority group.

Few parents are likely to object, nowadays, if their daughters want to become professional dancers. At least, they do not object for other than practical reasons. Considering the employment opportunities for even the best dancers, they are right to wonder whether their daughters will get enough work to qualify for unemployment benefits in off-seasons. (This, it must be understood, is to approach the peak of security in the American dance world.)

With sons, it remains a different story. Too often, boys who want to dance are still regarded apprehensively by their fathers. This is not necessarily because the fathers object so much. After all, they know that dancing is a thoroughly manly activity. No, what a father probably worries about most is what people will think or say if his son takes up dancing.

Still, the national attitude about the dance is far more relaxed than it was as recently as twenty-five years ago, and this relaxation has contributed to the democratization as well as the increase in size of the dance public.

The freer feeling probably results largely from the public's increased exposure to the dance and the easy familiarity the increase has induced. In the last two decades, for example, serious dance has become a fairly frequent component of Broadway musicals and television programs. It has established itself in schools and colleges and has even been entertained hospitably in the White House.

We have not all suddenly become sophisticated dance patrons, and all of us never will. The truly discriminating public for any art has always been small and will always remain so. But, like any other art in this age, the dance must have the support of a mass public to keep it alive.

No one really believes that all who visit the Museum of Modern Art are connoisseurs of twentieth century painting and sculpture. But without a big paying public, the real connoisseurs would not have the museum as it now exists to visit, and contemporary painters themselves would be much the poorer in every way without the stimulation and advertising their art gets there.

Serious music lovers, performers and composers are equally dependent upon the patronage of a public that merely likes rather than lives by music. How much menu planning, daydreaming, even sleeping, go on in sight and sound of the New York Philharmonic and the Metropolitan Opera will never be known. But if the cooks, dreamers and sleepers were all to stay home, the orchestra and the opera would be out of business in a hurry.

When any art begins to cater consciously to the lowest common denominator of public taste merely to keep seats filled, the cause of the art is lost, of course. But it is the responsibility of artists and management to see that this does not happen. If it does happen, it is not the public's fault.

The dance is fortunate to be attracting a steadily increasing public, and if it uses the public's support to enrich the art at the highest levels, its future here should be bright.

GROWING PAINS OF A SHRINKING INDUSTRY [10]

"A little rebellion now and then," Thomas Jefferson once remarked, "is a good thing." He was referring to cataclysms "in the political and physical worlds" but his views are equally applicable to disturbances in other spheres. They are particularly relevant to our mass communication media, which require constant reassessment, revision, and an occasional revolution if they are adequately to fulfill their informational, educational, and entertainment functions.

In the past decade TV has done to the movies even as the movies in their precocious youth did to the legitimate theatre. Offering the public the ultimate in convenience, economy, and banal entertainment, almost overnight it cut motion picture theatre attendance in half. Ten thousand of the 22,000 old "hard top" theatres have been converted into supermarkets, bowling alleys, or garages. Formerly every major company-produced film made a profit unless it was unfortunately labeled "artistic" or "experimental." Today some 75 per cent of the pictures released are losing money. The huge studios, formerly exhibit A of

[10] From article by Arthur Mayer, author and motion picture producer. *Saturday Review.* 44:21-3+. F. 25, '61. Reprinted by permission.

Hollywood's hegemony, have become, like the dinosaur, too cumbersome to survive in a changed world, and the more prosperous companies are those unencumbered either by realty or by fealty to traditional production procedures. The picture makers who have been exhorted so often in the past to raise their sights may also have to raze their sites. Indeed, it is probable that eventually studio facilities will be rented by producers anywhere from Culver City to Capetown only if and when they are required.

Twelve years ago Hollywood appeared impregnably entrenched as the cinema capital of the world. The profits of its seven major producing companies were running over $200 million annually. Ninety million Americans, or so it was claimed by movie press agents (who rarely exaggerate more than 20 per cent), were attending motion pictures weekly. To satisfy their seemingly insatiable demands four hundred pictures were being mass-produced every year. The industry's mores as well as its movies were dictated by a handful of survivors from the pioneer days of dog-eat-dog who had proved most proficient at devouring rather than being devoured. They were men of incredible acumen, ambition, and avarice whose pre-eminence, rudely speaking, was attributable to their faith in sentimental, escapist entertainment and their lack of faith in the intelligence of the public. Of any social responsibility to portray the nation's needs realistically and to foster its faith in human dignity and democratic institutions they were utterly unaware. And yet, in spite of the commercialism and cynicism of Beverly Hills and Broadway and the readiness of Main Street to accept whatever film fodder it was proffered, so great is the vitality of the medium and the skill and dedication of its creators and craftsmen that every year a considerable number of films of genuine merit were produced.

Suddenly, however, the movie makers were faced with a form of competition unprecedented in industrial annals. Thirty-four million Americans, it is estimated, are looking at motion pictures every night but 28 million of them are watching them gratis in their living rooms rather than paying to see them in theatres. The ancient practice of regular weekly or twice-a-week attendance is as alien to the way of life of our young people (who constitute over 50 per cent of present theatre patronage) as wearing corsets or holding hands in the front parlor. It has been replaced by a more selective, though not necessarily a more discriminating, approach that confines theatre patronage to a limited number of productions which for reasons still undetermined stimulate the public's salivary entertainment glands. Some of the playing time formerly monopolized by Hollywood has now been pre-empted by foreign films—not primarily cinematic achievements of the caliber of *Wild Strawberries* or *Hiroshima, Mon Amour* but fatuous spectaculars like *Hercules*. Moreover, the industry's much-prized glamour is fading, it badly needs new personalities to replace the balding, face-lifted gods and goddesses of the forties, but the younger generation sometimes seems more productive of juvenile delinquents than of juvenile stars and starlets.

Confronted by such catastrophes, producers proceeded to bolster their dwindling bank accounts by disposing of their pre-'48 negatives to their TV competitors. In this fashion they inadvertently nullified the efforts of a few video craftsmen to develop their own indigenous art, at the same time demonstrating their complete indifference to their own cultural heritage by permitting the classics of their past to be shown nightly, brutally chopped and interlarded with paeans of praise for detergents, deodorants, dentifrices, and depilatories. "It was," said Spyros Skouras, president of Twentieth Century-Fox, "a tragic mistake." But Mr. Skouras, along with his fellow presidents, is now repeating the tragedy by selling his post-'48 features.

Indeed, it can safely be predicted that in a belated effort to make show biz businesslike, anything that the companies possess that is not nailed down, whether old films, old studios, or old relatives, will be jettisoned. It is also evident that they will resort to any form of diversification that promises to make a buck, such as the production of quickies for video, or calculating machines (colossal, of course) or toll-TV electronic devices designed to replace the theatre box office with a box office in every home.

Meanwhile, the movie executives proceeded with considerable courage, foresight, and ingenuity to revolutionize completely the processes and practices of picture making through five drastic reforms: (1) Old-fashioned major company assembly-line procedures were replaced by independent production; (2) an ever-increasing percentage of pictures was shot away from Hollywood, particularly on foreign locations; (3) the number of films produced annually was reduced by 50 per cent, with the bulk of the industry's resources and showmanship concentrated on unprecedentedly costly features known as blockbusters; (4) new widescreen processes were introduced; (5) story material for plots and dialogue supposedly more sophisticated and mature than had formerly been regarded as suitable for mass entertainment replaced the so-called family pictures, bucolic comedies, and saccharine romances. The future may be fraught with perils and complexities but we have at least said a final farewell on the theatre screen to Ma and Pa Kettle and to Francis, the talking mule. We have also, at least temporarily, said goodbye to the gravediggers who prematurely pronounced the industry on its deathbed. Theatre receipts in 1960 amounted to $1.375 million, a figure only barely exceeded in three halcyon years of the late forties, and the stocks of all of the major producers surged upward in a depressed Wall Street market.

Independent production, of course, is nothing new. Over the years such pioneers as Goldwyn and Selznick concentrated their activities on a limited number of pictures produced slowly with meticulous care. Naturally, the batting average of their product was considerably higher than that of the major companies which were each turning out some fifty-two pictures annually and which put a new production into work every week regardless of whether a suitable story, star, or director was available. Only one company, United Artists, founded by Chaplin, Pickford, Fairbanks, and Griffith, through the years operated exclusively as a distributor of independently made pictures. Of it, one industry wit wisecracked: "The lunatics have taken over the asylum."

The show-wise young attorneys who took over United Artists in 1951 after it had long teetered on the edge of bankruptcy were, however, far from lunatics. They reduced its overhead, undersold their competitors, ingratiated themselves with bankers, and enticed top-notch producers by extending them something previously unknown in the industry—almost complete autonomy. As a consequence of these innovations, with amazing speed they dispensed with red ink and within ten years were showing an annual profit of over $4 million.

Nothing is as persuasive to magnates, movie or otherwise, as a balance sheet which each year shows the assets increasingly outbalancing the liabilities. Today practically every other picture company has adopted to a substantial degree United Artists' production policies. This industry-wide acceptance was also accelerated by our tax laws, which make it more lucrative to be an entrepreneur who can pay a capital gain of 25 per cent on stock sales rather than a wage slave sweating beneath the yoke of a 90 per cent income tax. The good news spread rapidly among the unhappy upper-bracket set of the West Coast.

Independent production has failed, like most other panaceas, to live up to its advance publicity. In the case of a few gifted individuals such as Kramer, Spiegel, and Jerry Wald it has achieved a considerable advance in individual initiative and in freedom of subject matter and treatment. There is, however, a plethora of other independents no more encumbered by humanitarian or artistic ideals than were their big-studio predecessors. Certainly the 1960 record furnishes no occasion for complacency in American cinematic circles. In selecting the ten best pictures of the year the critics of *Saturday Review,* the New York *Post,* and the New York *Herald Tribune* included only two American pictures in their lists. Bosley Crowther expressed the sentiments of most of his confreres when he accused Hollywood of "extravagance, bad taste, and vulgarity."

Actually the major companies have practically abdicated their producing functions and are now primarily investors, distributors, and landlords. As investors they advance to independents all the finances required to make their pictures, receiving in return —depending upon whether they are dealing with John Doe or John Wayne—anywhere from 75 to 10 per cent of the profits, if any. They levy a fee of approximately 30 per cent for their distribution services, calculated to assure them a profit even on unprofitable pictures, and charge rent for their studios as and when they are used.

More and more films, however, are being made in alien locations formerly of little repute. The independents seem to have a special penchant for islands—the Canaries, Rhodes, Cyprus, even Manhattan. Approximately 40 per cent of the movies made or financed by the majors last year were shot abroad, and in spite of the wails of the West Coast unions the trend is certain to continue, and possibly to expand. The industry stumbled onto this bonanza more through good luck than good business judgment.

In the postwar years the only way it could utilize its unconvertible foreign currency earnings was to produce pictures where the funds were accumulating. Possibly because of the authenticity and the novelty of the locations, possibly because of increased American awareness of the charms of the Old World, possibly just because they were excellent pictures, such productions as *Three Coins in the Fountain, The Third Man,* and *Roman Holiday* proved, to everybody's surprise, to be smash hits. Generally speaking, production costs were and still are considerably less in such countries as Yugoslavia or Greece than at home. Extras for big spectaculars come a drachma a dozen, armies of rival nations compete for the glory of appearing in a blockbuster, and no sets need be constructed for ancient castles, awesome cathedrals, or authentic chateaux.

Moreover, there are special advantages to be gained from subsidies and preferential treatment provided by practically every government in the world except that of the U.S. for productions made within their borders and utilizing some of their native personnel. American producers have on occasion been sufficiently persuasive with local authorities to qualify for payments in three or four different countries! High-salaried performers took to foreign production like starlets to swimming pools. Some specialists in the role of the all-American boy, aged fifty or more, have resorted to the un-American expedient of numbered bank accounts in Switzerland that enable them to escape the clutches of the Collector of Internal Revenue while retaining their U.S. citizenship. Quite a few producers and directors aver that their artistic integrity and opportunity for self-expression are in direct proportion to their remoteness from Hollywood. More and more, these foreign-made films certainly represent the cream of the U.S. cinema crop. The 1956 Oscar was awarded to *Around the World in 80 Days,* surprisingly enough filmed around the world. The 1957 winner was *The Bridge on the River Kwai,* made in Ceylon. The Oscar for 1958 was voted to *Gigi,* shot to a large extent in France, and last year the award was given to *Ben-Hur,* made in Italy.

The independents, like their big-company predecessors, have displayed little zeal in developing literary material specifically designed for cinematic purposes but enormous energy in pursuing the rights for successful books and plays, frequently written by men whom Hollywood had previously hired and fired. Michener's *Hawaii* was sold prior to publication for $600,000. *The Sound of Music* was purchased for $1.25 million guaranteed against 10 per cent of the gross, and this percentage of the gross formula, whether applied to authors, actors or directors, can prove, to put it mildly, quite costly. Bill Holden, for instance, received 10 per cent of the gross of *The Bridge on the River Kwai*, and *The Bridge* will probably wind up with world-wide rentals of some $20 million. Hitchcock's *Psycho* deal for 75 per cent of the profits should net him over $5 million. Marlon Brando, when he is not producing pictures for his own company, prefers to gamble on 50 per cent of the picture's profits but he does not gamble very recklessly as he demands a guarantee of $750,000. . . .

Instead of seeking to develop new talent, a task that requires a readiness to sacrifice immediate profits for highly speculative future earnings, the present breed of producers prefers to experiment with wide-angle lenses, 70 mm. film, or batteries of cameras handling different parts of the over-all scene, designed to give greater depth, vision, and clarity. Anamorphic lenses, which can expand and subsequently compress the image on the negative, have been available since 1927 when Cinemascope (under another name) was first demonstrated by a French inventor. It attracted little attention, however, until television made it imperative to achieve greater dramatic effectiveness than any little box in the living room could possibly afford. These so-called new techniques are immensely effective in spectacular scenes like the chariot race in *Ben Hur*. On the other hand, the small attic in which Anne Frank and her family were hidden is now blown up to the size of Grand Central Station. Close-ups are frequently so magnified that susceptible patrons find themselves hypnotized by the pores of the heroine's nose or the gyrations of the hero's Adam's apple. As Cecil DeMille once said: "With VistaVision I can show the Hebrews crossing the Red Sea, but I cannot adequately portray the Madonna fondling the Christ child." Another producer, deploring the new "letter-box" proportions of the screen, complained that he could show Gulliver in Lilliput prone but never upright.

Moreover, these wide-screen processes add tremendously to picture-making costs already swollen by inflated salaries, story costs, and union demands. Last year only 224 pictures were released by American film distributors, but the total sum spent for their production and distribution was triple what it had been for the 368 pictures made in 1941. With the demise of block booking, movies entered the blockbuster ice age. The spectaculars, costing anywhere from $12 million to $15 million, are proving treasure troves with unprecedented world-wide grosses of $60 million to $70 million. Many of the baby blockbusters, budgeted for only a negligible $2 million to $5 million, are also doing quite nicely. Of the twenty-five highest-grossing pictures of all time, twenty-two have been released in the "depressed" years since 1950.

In sixty years of picture making we have, however, learned distressingly little about the qualities that make some pictures so popular and others so unpopular, not only from coast to coast but from continent to continent. In speaking of modern physics, the distinguished scientist Dr. Isador Rabi once said: "We work with known laws in the midst of data unknown and unknowable." Motion pictures face exactly the opposite quandary. We know the data but the laws we work with are apparently unknown and unknowable. Certainly the favorites of . . . [1960] fail to furnish more guidance. The top twelve as listed by *Variety*, the industry's weekly Bible, are as follows: *Ben-Hur*, the epic to end all epics; *Solomon and Sheba*, a minor-league epic whose historical inaccuracies and ostentatious bad taste gave rise to rumors that Cecil DeMille must still be alive; Hitchcock's *Psycho*, an inexpensive chiller-diller, which in time will probably prove the highest-grossing black-and-white negative since Griffith's *Birth of a Nation; Can-Can*, a musical which neither Khrushchev nor the critics, but only the public, seemed to like; *Operation Petticoat, The Apartment*, and *Please Don't Eat the Daisies*, three comedies chock-full of chuckles rather than belly laughs; two sex sizzlers, *Butterfield 8* and *From the Terrace*, and the sizzlier if not sexier *Suddenly Last Summer*, which Eric Johnston, a connoisseur of movies if not of erotica, testified that he had seen three times without detecting any suggestion of homosexuality; *On the Beach*, a message picture of the type which exhibitors have for years claimed should be circulated by Western Union and not in picture theatres, and *Ocean's 11*, which at the very time that all authorities were agreeing that star value was waning, owed its popularity to the presence in the cast of members of the so-called rat pack, Frank Sinatra, Dean Martin, and Peter Lawford. So much for the experts!

Although "controversial" is still a dirty word in the motion picture lexicon, "mature" is for the moment the password. Unfortunately, many producers apparently suffer from the immature delusion that mature pictures are exclusively those dealing with sex in its more sordid aspects. They seem to be unaware of the many dramatic situations in a dynamic, democratic society and in a rapidly changing world order worthy of cinematic attention besides seduction and promiscuity. Until recently motion pictures were subject to the strict surveillance of censor boards in some dozen states and over fifty municipalities. A series of Supreme Court decisions, however, has so undermined the scope and power of prerelease censorship that only five state boards still survive, and they rarely, if ever, ban a picture; at the most, they insist on a few comparatively inconsequential cuts. A handful of municipal boards still occasionally make a local nuisance of themselves but if Memphis, for example, condemns *The Lovers,* this only serves to stimulate the citizenry in large numbers to cross the river to East Memphis to see how wicked the picture might be—and to return home considerably disappointed. . . .

In the long run, where an open market prevails and where the public pays the bill as it does in movies but not in TV, the country will get as good art or entertainment as it deserves. Walt Whitman once wrote: "To have great poets there must be great audiences too." The same is true of motion pictures. A sluggish, apathetic people will be satisfied with sentimental, escapist movies. A strong, virile nation will demand and receive films warm with insight, tenderness, and power. . . .

Personally, I am a corrigible optimist, by which I mean I believe that we are making progress but making it in these critical times far too slowly and too intermittently. The old Mencken dictum that "no one ever went broke underestimating the taste of the American public" is still true, but it is also true that money can be made by having faith in the taste of a substantial segment of the public. It is a long stride forward from the dramatic and musical Broadway hits of my youth such as *Abie's Irish Rose* and *Capt. Jinks of the Horse Marines* to *The Miracle Worker* and *My Fair Lady.* I have no brief for the current best-sellers, such as *Hawaii* and *Advise and Consent,* but surely they represent an improvement in subject matter and skill over *Three Weeks* and *When Knighthood Was in Flower.* More Americans are attending concerts than baseball games and over the weekends the art museums are scarcely capable of accommodating the crowds. It is unfortunate that our most popular current movies fail to indicate similar progress in cinematic taste but the fine reception extended to some comparatively inexpensive English pictures such as *Room at the Top, I'm All Right, Jack, The Mouse That Roared,* and *Tunes of Glory* is at least an encouraging symptom.

Looking back over the past decade, the movie executives (at least those who know their Shakespeare) can with pardonable pride say with Hotspur: "Out of this nettle, danger, we pluck this flower, safety." But while they have been preoccupied with plucking the flower, their old-time laurels have been withering. Surely it is not enough for any medium of communication to be safe in a world which calls for courage, beauty, gaiety, and truth.

PROGRAM CONTROL: THE BROADCASTERS ARE PUBLIC TRUSTEES [11]

Governor Collins, Distinguished Guests, Ladies and Gentlemen: Thank you for this opportunity to meet with you today. This is my first public address since I took over my new job. When the New Frontiersmen rode into town, I locked myself in my office to do my homework and get my feet wet. But apparently I haven't managed to stay out of hot water. I seem to have detected a certain nervous apprehension about what I might say or do when I emerged from that locked office for this, my maiden station break.

First, let me begin by dispelling a rumor. I was not picked for this job because I regard myself as the fastest draw on the New Frontier.

Second, let me start a rumor. Like you, I have carefully read President Kennedy's messages about the regulatory agencies, conflict of interest, and the dangers of *ex parte* contacts. And of course, we at the Federal Communications Commission will

[11] From address by Newton N. Minow, former chairman, Federal Communications Commission, delivered to the 39th Annual Convention of the National Association of Broadcasters, Washington, D.C., May 9, 1961. In *Vital Speeches of the Day.* 27:533-37. Je. 15, '61. Reprinted by permission.

do our part. Indeed, I may even suggest that we change the name of the FCC to The Seven Untouchables!

It may also come as a surprise to some of you, but I want you to know that you have my admiration and respect. Yours is a most honorable profession. Anyone who is in the broadcasting business has a tough row to hoe. You earn your bread by using public property. When you work in broadcasting you volunteer for public service, public pressure, and public regulation. You must compete with other attractions and other investments, and the only way you can do it is to prove to us every three years that you should have been in business in the first place.

I can think of easier ways to make a living.

But I cannot think of more satisfying ways.

I admire your courage—but that doesn't mean I would make life any easier for you. Your license lets you use the public's airwaves as trustees for 180 million Americans. The public is your beneficiary. If you want to stay on as trustees, you must deliver a decent return to the public—not only to your stockholders. So, as a representative of the public, your health and your product are among my chief concerns.

As to your health: let's talk only of television today. 1960 gross broadcast revenues of the television industry were over $1,268,000,000; profit before taxes was $243,900,000, an average return on revenue of 19.2 per cent. Compared with 1959, gross broadcast revenues were $1,163,900,000, and profit before taxes was $222,300,000, an average return on revenue of 19.1 per cent. So, the percentage increase of total revenues from 1959 to 1960 was 9 per cent, and the percentage increase of profit was 9.7 per cent. This, despite a recession. For your investors, the price has indeed been right.

I have confidence in your health.

But not in your product.

It is with this and much more in mind that I come before you today.

One editorialist in the trade press wrote that "the FCC of the New Frontier is going to be one of the toughest FCC's in the history of broadcast regulation." If he meant that we intend to enforce the law in the public interest, let me make it perfectly clear that he is right—we do.

If he meant that we intend to muzzle or censor broadcasting, he is dead wrong.

It would not surprise me if some of you had expected me to come here today and say in effect, "Clean up your own house or the Government will do it for you."

Well, in a limited sense, you would be right—I've just said it.

But I want to say to you earnestly that it is not in that spirit that I come before you today, nor is it in that spirit that I intend to serve the FCC.

I am in Washington to help broadcasting, not to harm it; to strengthen it, not weaken it; to reward it, not punish it; to encourage it, not threaten it; to stimulate it, not censor it.

Above all, I am here to uphold and protect the public interest.

What do we mean by "the public interest"? Some say the public interest is merely what interests the public.

I disagree.

So does your distinguished president, Governor [LeRoy] Collins [former governor of Florida]. In a recent speech he said,

> Broadcasting to serve the public interest, must have a soul and a conscience, a burning desire to excel, as well as to sell; the urge to build the character, citizenship and intellectual stature of people, as well as to expand the gross national product. . . . By no means do I imply that broadcasters disregard the public interest. . . . But a much better job can be done, and should be done.

I could not agree more.

And I would add that in today's world, with chaos in Laos and the Congo aflame, with Communist tyranny on our Caribbean doorstep and relentless pressure on our Atlantic alliance, with social and economic problems at home of the gravest nature, yes, and with technological knowledge that makes it possible, as our President has said, not only to destroy our world but to destroy poverty around the world—in a time of peril and opportunity, the old complacent, unbalanced fare of action-adventure and situation comedies is simply not good enough.

Your industry possesses the most powerful voice in America. It has an inescapable duty to make that voice ring with intelligence and with leadership. In a few years, this exciting industry has grown from a novelty to an instrument of overwhelming impact on the American people. It should be making ready for the kind of leadership that newspapers and magazines assumed years ago, to make our people aware of their world.

Ours has been called the jet age, the atomic age, the space age. It is also, I submit, the television age. And just as history will decide whether the leaders of today's world employed the atom to destroy the world or rebuild it for mankind's benefit, so will history decide whether today's broadcasters employed their powerful voice to enrich the people or debase them.

If I seem today to address myself chiefly to the problems of television, I don't want any of you radio broadcasters to think we've gone to sleep at your switch—we haven't. We still listen. But in recent years most of the controversies and crosscurrents in broadcast programing have swirled around television. And so my subject today is the television industry and the public interest.

Like everybody, I wear more than one hat. I am the chairman of the FCC. I am also a television viewer and the husband and father of other television viewers. I have seen a great many television programs that seemed to me eminently worth while, and I am not talking about the much-bemoaned good old days of *Playhouse 90* and *Studio One*.

I am talking about this past season. Some were wonderfully entertaining, such as *The Fabulous Fifties*, the *Fred Astaire Show*, and the *Bing Crosby Special;* some were dramatic and moving, such as Conrad's *Victory* and *Twilight Zone;* some were marvelously informative, such as *The Nation's Future, CBS Reports,* and *The Valiant Years.* I could list many more—programs that I am sure everyone here felt enriched his own life and that of his family. When television is good, nothing—not the theatre, not the magazines or newspapers—nothing is better.

But when television is bad, nothing is worse. I invite you to sit down in front of your television set when your station goes on the air and stay there without a book, magazine, newspaper, profit and loss sheet or rating book to distract you—and keep your eyes glued to that set until the station signs off. I can assure you that you will observe a vast wasteland.

You will see a procession of game shows, violence, audience participation shows, formula comedies about totally unbelievable families, blood and thunder, mayhem, violence, sadism, murder, western badmen, western good men, private eyes, gangsters, more violence, and cartoons. And, endlessly, commercials—many screaming, cajoling, and offending. And most of all, boredom. True, you will see a few things you will enjoy. But they will be very, very few. And if you think I exaggerate, try it.

Is there one person in this room who claims that broadcasting can't do better?

Well, a glance at next season's proposed programing can give us little heart. Of 73½ hours of prime evening time, the networks have tentatively scheduled 59 hours to categories of action-adventure, situation comedy, variety, quiz, and movies.

Is there one network president in this room who claims he can't do better?

Well, is there at least one network president who believes that the other networks can't do better?

Gentlemen, your trust accounting with your beneficiaries is overdue.

Never have so few owed so much to so many.

Why is so much of television so bad? I have heard many answers: demands of your advertisers; competition for ever higher ratings; the need always to attract a mass audience; the high cost of television programs; the insatiable appetite for programing material—these are some of them. Unquestionably, these are tough problems not susceptible to easy answers.

But I am not convinced that you have tried hard enough to solve them.

I do not accept the idea that the present over-all programing is aimed accurately at the public taste. The ratings tell us only that some people have their television sets turned on and of that number, so many are tuned to one channel and so many to another. They don't tell us what the public might watch if they were offered half a dozen additional choices. A rating, at best, is an indication of how many people saw what you gave them. Unfortunately, it does not reveal the depth of the penetration, or the intensity of reaction, and it never reveals what the acceptance would have been if what you gave them had been better—if all the forces of art and creativity and daring and imagination had been unleashed. I believe in the people's good sense and good taste, and I am not convinced that the people's taste is as low as some of you assume.

My concern with the rating services is not with their accuracy. Perhaps they are accurate. I really don't know. What, then, is wrong with the ratings? It's not been their accuracy—it's been their use.

Certainly, I hope you will agree that ratings should have little influence where children are concerned. The best estimates indicate that during the hours of 5 to 6 P.M. 60 per cent of your audience is composed of children under 12. And most young children today, believe it or not, spend as much time watching television as they do in the schoolroom. I repeat—let that sink in—most young children today spend as much time watching television as they do in the schoolroom. It used to be said that there were three great influences on a child: home, school, and church. Today, there is a fourth great influence, and you ladies and gentlemen control it.

If parents, teachers, and ministers conducted their responsibilities by following the ratings, children would have a steady diet of ice cream, school holidays, and no Sunday school. What about your responsibilities? Is there no room on television to teach, to inform, to uplift, to stretch, to enlarge the capacities of our children? Is there no room for programs deepening their understanding of children in other lands? Is there no room for a children's news show explaining something about the world to them at their level of understanding? Is there no room for reading the great literature of the past, teaching them the great traditions of freedom? There are some fine children's shows, but they are drowned out in the massive doses of cartoons, violence, and more violence. Must these be your trademarks? Search your consciences and see if you cannot offer more to your young beneficiaries whose future you guide so many hours each and every day.

What about adult programing and ratings? You know, newspaper publishers take popularity ratings too. The answers are pretty clear: it is almost always the comics, followed by the advice to the lovelorn columns. But, ladies and gentlemen, the news is still on the front page of all newspapers, the editorials are not replaced by more comics, the newspapers have not become one long collection of advice to the lovelorn. Yet newspapers do not need a license from the Government to be in business—they do not use public property. But in television—where your responsibilities as public trustees are so plain, the moment that the ratings indicate that westerns are popular there are new imitations of westerns on the air faster than the old coaxial cable could take us from Hollywood to New York. Broadcasting cannot continue to live by the numbers. Ratings ought to be the slave of the broadcaster, not his master. And you and I both know that the rating services themselves would agree.

Let me make clear that what I am talking about is balance. I believe that the public interest is made up of many interests. There are many people in this great country and you must serve all of us. You will get no argument from me if you say that, given a choice between a western and a symphony, more people will watch the western. I like westerns and private eyes too— but a steady diet for the whole country is obviously not in the public interest. We all know that people would more often prefer to be entertained than stimulated or informed. But your obligations are not satisfied if you look only to popularity as a test of what to broadcast. You are not only in show business; you are free to communicate ideas as well as relaxation. You must provide a wider range of choices, more diversity, more alternatives. It is not enough to cater to the nation's whims— you must also serve the nation's needs.

And I would add this—that if some of you persist in a relentless search for the highest rating and the lowest common denominator, you may very well lose your audience. Because, to paraphrase a great American who was recently my law partner, the people are wise, wiser than some of the broadcasters—and politicians—think.

As you may have gathered, I would like to see television improved. But how is this to be brought about? By voluntary action by the broadcasters themselves? By direct Government intervention? Or how?

Let me address myself now to my role not as a viewer but as chairman of the FCC. I could not if I would chart for you this afternoon in detail all of the actions I contemplate. Instead, I want to make clear some of the fundamental principles which guide me.

First: the people own the air. They own it as much in prime evening time as they do at 6 o'clock Sunday morning. For every hour that the people give you—you owe them something. I intend to see that your debt is paid with service.

Second: I think it would be foolish and wasteful for us to continue any worn-out wrangle over the problems of payola, rigged quiz shows, and other mistakes of the past. There are laws on the books which we will enforce. But there is no chip on my shoulder. We live together in perilous, uncertain times; we face together staggering problems; and we must not waste much time now by rehashing the clichés of past controversy. To quarrel over the past is to lose the future.

Third: I believe in the free enterprise system. I want to see broadcasting improved and I want you to do the job. I am proud to champion your cause. It is not rare for American businessmen to serve a public trust. Yours is a special trust because it is imposed by law.

Fourth: I will do all I can to help educational television. There are still not enough educational stations, and major centers of the country still lack usable educational channels. If there were a limited number of printing presses in this country, you may be sure that a fair proportion of them would be put to educational use. Educational television has an enormous contribution to make to the future, and I intend to give it a hand along the way. If there is not a nationwide educational television system in this country, it will not be the fault of the FCC.

Fifth: I am unalterably opposed to governmental censorship. There will be no suppression of programing which does not meet with bureaucratic tastes. Censorship strikes at the tap root of our free society.

Sixth: I did not come to Washington to idly observe the squandering of the public's airwaves. The squandering of our airwaves is no less important than the lavish waste of any precious natural resource. I intend to take the job of chairman of the FCC very seriously. I believe in the gravity of my own particular sector of the New Frontier. There will be times perhaps when you will consider that I take myself or my job *too* seriously. Frankly, I don't care if you do. For I am convinced that either one takes this job seriously—or one can be seriously taken.

Now, how will these principles be applied? Clearly, at the heart of the FCC's authority lies its power to license, to renew or fail to renew, or to revoke a license. As you know, when your license comes up for renewal, your performance is compared with your promises. I understand that many people feel that in the past licenses were often renewed *pro forma*. I say to you now: renewal will not be *pro forma* in the future. There is nothing permanent or sacred about a broadcast license.

But simply matching promises and performance is not enough. I intend to do more. I intend to find out whether the people care. I intend to find out whether the community which each broadcaster serves believes he has been serving the public interest. When a renewal is set down for hearing, I intend—wherever possible—to hold a well-advertised public hearing, right in the community you have promised to serve. I want the people who own the air and the homes that television enters to tell you and the FCC what's been going on. I want the people—if they are truly interested in the service you give them—to make notes, document cases, tell us the facts. For those few of you who really believe that the public interest is merely what interests the public—I hope that these hearings will arouse no little interest.

The FCC has a fine reserve of monitors—almost 180 million Americans gathered around 56 million sets. If you want those monitors to be your friends at court—it's up to you. . . .

I join Governor Collins in his views so well expressed to the advertisers who use the public air. I urge the networks to join him and undertake a very special mission on behalf of this industry: you can tell your advertisers, "This is the high quality we are going to serve—take it or other people will. If you think you can find a better place to move automobiles, cigarettes and soap—go ahead and try."

Tell your sponsors to be less concerned with costs per thousand and more concerned with understanding per million. And remind your stockholders that an investment in broadcasting is buying a share in public responsibility.

The networks can start this industry on the road to freedom from the dictatorship of numbers.

But there is more to the problem than network influences on stations or advertiser influences on networks. I know the problems networks face in trying to clear some of their best programs—the informational programs that exemplify public service. They are your finest hours—whether sustaining or commercial, whether regularly scheduled or special—these are the signs that broadcasting knows the way to leadership. They make the public's trust in you a wise choice.

They should be seen. As you know, we are readying for use new forms by which broadcast stations will report their programing to the Commission. You probably also know that special attention will be paid in these reports to public service programing. I believe that stations taking network service should also be required to report the extent of the local clearance of network public service programing, and when they fail to clear them, they should explain why. If it is to put on some outstanding local program, this is one reason. But, if it is simply to carry some old movie, that is an entirely different matter. The Commission should consider such clearance reports carefully when making up its mind about the licensee's over-all programing. . . .

We have approved an experiment with pay TV, and in New York we are testing the potential of UHF broadcasting. Either or both of these may revolutionize television. Only a foolish prophet would venture to guess the direction they will take, and their effect. But we intend that they shall be explored fully—for they are part of broadcasting's New Frontier.

The questions surrounding pay TV are largely economic. The questions surrounding UHF are largely technological. We are going to give the infant pay TV a chance to prove whether it can offer a useful service; we are going to protect it from those who would strangle it in its crib. . . .

Another and perhaps the most important frontier: television will rapidly join the parade into space. International television will be with us soon. No one knows how long it will be until a broadcast from a studio in New York will be viewed in India as well as in Indiana, will be seen in the Congo as it is seen in Chicago. But as surely as we are meeting here today, that day will come—and once again our world will shrink.

What will the people of other countries think of us when they see our western badmen and good men punching each other in the jaw in between the shooting? What will the Latin American or African child learn of America from our great communications industry? We cannot permit television in its present form to be our voice overseas.

There is your challenge to leadership. You must re-examine some fundamentals of your industry. You must open your minds and open your hearts to the limitless horizons of tomorrow.

I can suggest some words that should serve to guide you:

Television and all who participate in it are jointly accountable to the American public for respect for the special needs of children, for community responsibility, for the advancement of education and culture, for the acceptability of the program materials chosen, for decency and decorum in production, and for propriety in advertising. This responsibility cannot be discharged by any given group of programs, but can be discharged only through the highest standards of respect for the American home, applied to every moment of every program presented by television.

Program materials should enlarge the horizons of the viewer, provide him with wholesome entertainment, afford helpful stimulation, and remind him of the responsibilities which the citizen has towards his society.

These words are not mine. They are yours. They are taken literally from your own Television Code. They reflect the leadership and aspirations of your own great industry. I urge you to respect them as I do. . . .

We need imagination in programing, not sterility; creativity, not imitation; experimentation, not conformity; excellence, not mediocrity. Television is filled with creative, imaginative people. You must strive to set them free.

Television in its young life has had many hours of greatness —its *Victory at Sea,* its Army-McCarthy hearings, its *Peter Pan,* its *Kraft Theaters,* its *See It Now,* its *Project 20,* the World Series, its political conventions and campaigns, the Great Debates—and it has had its endless hours of mediocrity and its moments of public disgrace. There are estimates that today the average viewer spends about two hundred minutes daily with television, while the average reader spends thirty-eight minutes with magazines and forty minutes with newspapers. Television has grown faster than a teen-ager, and now it is time to grow up.

What you gentlemen broadcast through the people's air affects the people's taste, their knowledge, their opinions, their understanding of themselves and of their world, and their future.

The power of instantaneous sight and sound is without precedent in mankind's history. This is an awesome power. It has limitless capabilities for good—and for evil. And it carries with it awesome responsibilities, responsibilities which you and I cannot escape.

In his stirring Inaugural Address our President said, "And so, my fellow Americans: ask not what your country can do for you —ask what you can do for your country."

Ladies and Gentlemen:

Ask not what broadcasting can do for you. Ask what you can do for broadcasting.

I urge you to put the people's airwaves to the service of the people and the cause of freedom. You must help prepare a generation for great decisions. You must help a great nation fulfill its future.

Do this, and I pledge you our help.

PARALLEL PATHS [12]

The mass media are tempting targets: they are big, they are conspicuous, they are easily distorted, they invite bright and brittle condemnations—and they do have built-in limitations of their virtues. They have shown themselves inefficient warriors, and on the whole have tended to be too little concerned with what the intellectuals have had to say.

On the other side, the fondest attachment of the intellectuals is to theory not to practice; more importantly, there is among many intellectuals an uncongeniality with some of the basic ingredients of a democratic society and, in many cases, a real distrust of them. Democratic procedures, to some extent even democratic values, necessarily involve quantitative considerations, about which intellectuals are always uneasy. This uneasiness is not restricted to cultural matters. For example, it influences their view of the legislative processes and of economic interplays in our society. The intellectual is highly impatient of much that is imperfect but also inevitable in democracies. But despite these differences between intellectuals and the mass media, I think that they have something in common, that their efforts are fundamentally going toward the same general goal but along different paths.

[12] Article by Frank Stanton, president of the Columbia Broadcasting System. *Daedalus: Journal of the American Academy of Arts and Sciences.* 89:347-53. Spr. '60. Reprinted by permission.

I take it to be the distinguishing characteristic of civilized man that he is concerned with the environment and destiny of himself and his kind. The end of all scholarship, all art, all science, is the increase of knowledge and of understanding. The rubrics of scholarship have no inherent importance except in making the expansion of knowledge easier by creating system and order and catholicity. The freedom of the arts has no inherent value except in its admitting unlimited comments upon life and the materials of life. There is no *mystique* about science; its sole wonder exists in its continuous expansion of both the area and the detail of man's comprehension of his physical being and his surroundings.

The ultimate use of all man's knowledge and his art and his science cannot be locked up into little compartments to which only the initiate hold the keys. It cannot be contemplated solely by closeted groups, or imposed from above. If vitality is to be a force in the general life of mankind, it must sooner or later reach all men and enter into the general body of awarenesses. The advancement of the human lot consists in more people being aware of more, knowing more, understanding more.

The mass media believe in the broad dissemination of as much as can be comprehended by as many as possible. They employ techniques to arrest attention, to recruit interest, to lead their audiences into new fields. Often they must sacrifice detail or annotation for the sake of the general idea.

Although it may be presumptuous, perhaps I can suggest a general contrast in the position of the professional intellectual: he feels that knowledge, art, and understanding are all precious commodities that ought not to be diluted. He believes that if things were left to him this dilution would not happen, because the doors of influence would be closed to the inadequately educated until they had earned the right to open them, just as he did. His view is that if standards remain beyond the reach of the many, the general level will gradually rise.

In this respect, I dissent from Mr. [Leo] Rosten's conclusion [*Daedalus*. Spr. '60] that the intellectuals "project their own tastes, yearnings, and values upon the masses." I do not believe there is such an irreducible gap between the tastes, yearnings, and values of the intellectuals and those of the masses. The difficulty is that the intellectuals do not project at all to the uninitiated.

Their hope is to attract them, providing that it is not too many, too fast. They would wait for more and more people to qualify to the higher group, although they themselves want to stay a little ahead of the new arrivals.

This accounts, I believe, for the intellectuals' fear of popularization. The history of the Book-of-the-Month Club illustrates this point. Intellectuals have repeatedly made statements (not entirely characterized by a disciplined array of evidence), that the book club would bring about an "emasculation of the human mind whereby everyone loses the power of his determination in reading," and that the club's selections were "in many cases, not even an approximation to what the average intelligent reader wants." Yet a study by a Columbia University researcher found that over an eighteen-year span the reaction of reviewers, critics, and professors to the Book-of-the-Month Club selections was far higher in terms of approval than their reaction to random samples of nonselections.

By comparing the two heaviest book selections of the club in 1927 to their two lightest ones in 1949 (without other evidence) Stanley Edgar Hyman suggests [*Daedalus*. Spr. '60] that the standards of selection are deteriorating. Yet he makes no mention of the fact that in 1949 the Book-of-the-Month Club for the first time in its history distributed a serious contemporary play, *Death of a Salesman*, that it distributed a serious discussion of a vital issue in Vannevar Bush's *Modern Arms and Free Men*, that it put into hundreds of thousands of homes William Edward Langer's *Encyclopedia of World History*, that it brought to its subscribers George Orwell's *Nineteen Eighty-four*, Winston Churchill's *Their Finest Hour*, and A. B. Guthrie's Pulitzer Prize novel, *The Way West*.

Let me press what Mr. Hyman regards as evidence of "deterioration" of the Book-of-the-Month Club selections to the conclusion at which he himself arrived, that in the decade since 1949 "the selections seem to have continued to deteriorate." Even a glance at the evidence would refute this slashing generality. Indeed, the books distributed by the club throughout the 1950's suggest some high levels of excellence: in fiction there have been three books by William Faulkner, three by James Gould Cozzens, two by John Hersey, seven plays by Shaw, six by Thornton Wilder, Eugene O'Neill's *Long Day's Journey into Night*, novels by

Feuchtwanger, Salinger, Thomas Mann, Hemingway, John Cheever, and James Agee; there have been eight historical works by Churchill, two by Schlesinger, two by Van Wyck Brooks, others by Morison and Nevins, Dumas Malone, Bernard DeVoto, Catherine Drinker Bowen's life of John Adams, Toynbee's *Study of History*, two of Edith Hamilton's studies of ancient Greece, and Max Lerner's *American Civilization;* in poetry, Stephen Vincent Benét, and *The Oxford Book of American Verse;* from the classics, Bulfinch's *The Age of Fable*, Frazer's *The Golden Bough*, the Hart edition of Shakespeare, a new translation of *The Odyssey*, works by Dostoevsky, Gustave Flaubert, and Mark Twain; in art, Francis Henry Taylor's *Fifty Centuries of Art*, John Walker's *Masterpieces of Painting from the National Gallery*, and *Art Treasures of the Louvre;* in reference works, Fowler's *Modern English Usage*, Palmer's *Atlas of World History*, Audubon's *Birds*, and Evans' *Dictionary of Contemporary American Usage*.

To turn to television, I hear over and over such generalities as, "There is nothing but westerns on television," or "Television is all mysteries and blood and thunder." Such charges usually come from people who do not look at television, but that does not modify their position. As in the case just cited, there is no uncertainty about this exaggeration; one can look at the actual record.

Let us take by way of example the week of February 15 to 21, 1959, on the CBS Television Network, because that week had nothing exceptional about it. During the preceding week, there were such outstanding broadcasts as Tolstoy's *Family Happiness* and a repetition of the distinguished documentary, *The Face of Red China*. In the following week, the programs included the New York Philharmonic and the Old Vic Company's *Hamlet*. Returning to the unexceptional week of February 15, about $4\frac{1}{2}$ hours, or 1/18 of CBS Television's total program content of $75\frac{1}{2}$ hours, were devoted to westerns; about 5 hours, or 1/15, were taken up by mysteries. On the other hand, $7\frac{3}{4}$ hours, or about 1/10 of the total number of hours, were devoted to news and public affairs. Altogether, some 78 per cent of the evening programing was occupied by drama, fairly evenly divided among serious, comedy, mystery, westerns, and romance-adventure.

Looking at the record for the first five months of 1959, I find on the CBS Television Network alone four Philharmonic concerts; 90-minute-long productions of plays by Shakespeare, Barrie, and Saroyan, adaptations of Shaw and Ibsen, full-length productions of *The Browning Version,* Melville's *Billy Budd,* Henry James' *Wings of the Dove,* Hemingway's *For Whom the Bell Tolls,* and many distinguished original dramas; thirteen conversations with people of such diverse minds and talents as James Conant, Sir Thomas Beecham, and James Thurber; nine historic surveys of great personalities or developments of the twentieth century; and nine specially scheduled programs inquiring into major issues in public affairs, such as the Cuban revolution, the closing of integrated high schools, statehood for Hawaii, and the Geneva Conference.

I am citing these for two purposes. One is to show how, by using selected examples, it can be as easily proved that television is exclusively instructive as that it is exclusively diverting. My other purpose is by way of considering a practical response to the complaints that the intellectuals voice about all the mass media.

What do the intellectuals really want? Do they want us to do *only* serious programing, only programs of profound cultural value? Or do they just want us to do more? And if so, what is more? Do they want the Book-of-the-Month Club to distribute only heavy reading, or just more? Does the club do harm because it has included books of humor among the thirty to forty selections, alternates, and dividends it distributes each year? Is there any serious belief anywhere that among the paperback books we ought to censor what we consider culturally insignificant and allow only what we consider culturally enriching? Or do not the intellectuals really want to stake out reserves, admission to which would be granted only on their terms, in their way, at their pleasure?

Television occupies the air waves under the franchise of the American people. It has a threefold function: the dissemination of information, culture, and entertainment. There are different levels and different areas of interest at which these are sought by 150 million people. It is our purpose—and our endlessly tantalizing task—to make certain that we have enough of every area at every level of interest to hold the attention of significant segments of the public at one time or another. Therefore we do have programs more likely to be of interest to the intellectuals than to others. We can try to include everybody somewhere in our program planning, but we cannot possibly aim all the time only at the largest possible audience.

The practice of sound television programing is the same as the practice of any sound editorial operation. It involves always anticipating (if you can) and occasionally leading your subscribers or readers or audience. The "mass of consumers" does not decide, in the sense that it initiates programs, but it does respond to our decisions. A mass medium survives when it maintains a satisfactory batting average on affirmative responses, and it goes down when negative responses are too numerous or too frequent. But so also does the magazine with a circulation of five thousand —as the high mortality rate of the "little magazines" testifies. Success in editing, whether a mass medium or an esoteric quarterly, consists in so respecting the audience that one labors to bring to it something that meets an interest, a desire, or a need that has still to be completely filled. Obviously, the narrower and the more intellectually homogeneous your audience, the easier this is to do; and conversely, the larger it is and the more heterogeneous, the more difficult.

I must dissent from the unqualified charge that "advertisers today . . . exercise their most pernicious influence in television." The basis of this charge is that, while an advertiser buys space in a magazine with no power of choice as to the editorial content of the magazine, on television he allegedly controls both the commercials and what program goes into the time space. The matter is not so simple.

In the first place I categorically assert that no news or public-affairs program at CBS, however expensive to the sponsor, has ever been subject to his control, influence, or approval. There is a total and absolute independence in this respect.

An advertiser in magazines does have the power to associate his advertising with editorial content by his choice of a magazine. If he makes a household detergent, he can choose a magazine whose appeal is to housewives. In television, he can achieve this association only by seeking out kinds of programs, or, more properly, the kinds of audience to which specific programs appeal. This is of course why a razor blade company wants to sponsor sports programs. But this does not mean that the company is going to referee the game or coach the team. In television, for the most part, advertisers are sold programs by networks or by independent producers, somewhat in the sense that space in the magazines is sold by sales efforts based on the kind of audience the magazine reaches. At the same time, we are perfectly aware that in the rapid growth of television the problem of the advertiser's relationship with program content has not yet been satisfactorily solved. It is an area to which we are going to have to devote more thought and evolve new approaches.

I return to a central point: that some sort of hostility on the part of the intellectuals toward the mass media is inevitable, because the intellectuals are a minority, one not really reconciled to some basic features of democratic life. They are an articulate and cantankerous minority, not readily given to examining evidence about the mass media and then arriving at conclusions, but more likely to come to conclusions and then select the evidence to support them. But they are an invaluable minority. We all do care what they think because they are a historic force on which our society must always rely for self-examination and advancement. They constitute the outposts of our intellectual life as a people, they probe around frontiers in their splendid sparsity, looking around occasionally to see where—how far behind—the rest of us are. We are never going to catch up, but at least we shall always have somewhere to go.

As for the mass media, they are always in the process of trying, and they never really find the answers. They also are the victims of their pressing preoccupations, and can undoubtedly improve their performances, better understand their own roles, learn more rapidly. I feel that intellectuals and the media could really serve one another better if both parties informed themselves more fully, brought somewhat more sympathy to each other's examinations, and stopped once in a while to redefine their common goals. We in the mass media have probably been negligent in not drawing the intellectuals more intimately into our counsels, and the intellectuals, by and large, have not studied the evidence carefully enough before discussing the mass media. The mass media need the enlightened criticism, the thorough examination, of the intellectuals. When the latter are willing to promise these, we shall all make progress faster and steadier.

BIBLIOGRAPHY

An asterisk (*) preceding a reference indicates that the article or a part of it has been reprinted in this book.

BOOKS, PAMPHLETS, AND DOCUMENTS

Barzun, Jacques. House of intellect. Harper. New York. '59.

Boorstin, D. J. America and the image of Europe; reflections on American thought. Meridian. New York. '60.

Boroff, David. Campus U.S.A.; portraits of American colleges in action. Harper. New York. '61.

*Brogan, D. W. America in the modern world. Rutgers University Press. New Brunswick, N.J. '60.

Bruckberger, R. L. Image of America. Viking. New York. '59.

Chase, Richard. Democratic vista: a dialogue on life and letters in contemporary America. Doubleday. Garden City, N.Y. '58.

*Cordell, R. A. and Matson, Lowell. Off-Broadway theatre. Random House. New York. '59.

Denney, Reuel. Astonished muse. University of Chicago Press. Chicago. '57.

Fischer, John and Silvers, R. B. eds. Writing in America. Rutgers University Press. New Brunswick, N.J. '60.

Fortune Magazine. America in the sixties: the economy and the society. Harper (Torchbooks). New York. '60.
   Original title: Markets of the sixties. Harper. New York. '60.

Freedman, Leonard and Cotter, C. P. eds. Issues of the sixties. Wadsworth. San Francisco. '61.

Frohock, W. M. Strangers to this ground: cultural diversity in contemporary American writing. Southern Methodist University Press. Dallas. '61.

Galbraith, J. K. Affluent society. Houghton. Boston. '58.

Gardiner, H. C. In all conscience: reflections on books and culture. Hanover House. New York. '59.

*Gassner, John. Theatre at the crossroads. Holt. New York. '60.

Goodman, Paul. Growing up absurd; problems of youth in the organized system. Random House. New York. '60.

Griffith, Thomas. Waist-high culture. Harper. New York. '59.

Haydn, Hiram and Saunders, Betsy, eds. American Scholar reader. Atheneum. New York. '60.

Heckscher, August. Public happiness. Atheneum. New York. '62.

Hofstadter, Richard. Anti-intellectualism in American life. Knopf. New York. '63.

Huszar, G. B. de, ed. Intellectuals: a controversial portrait. Free Press. Glencoe, Ill. '60.

Jacobs, Norman, ed. Culture for the millions? Van Nostrand. Princeton, N.J. '61.

Jones, H. M. One great society: humane learning in the United States. Harcourt. New York. '59.

Kerr, Walter. Decline of pleasure. Simon and Schuster. New York. '62.

Klapper, J. T. Effects of mass media. Columbia University. Bureau of Applied Social Research. New York. '49.

Krutch, J. W. Human nature and the human condition. Random House. New York. '59.

Kwiat, J. J. and Turpie, M. C. eds. Studies in American culture; dominant ideas and images. University of Minnesota Press. Minneapolis. '60.

Larrabee, Eric. Self-conscious society. Doubleday. Garden City, N.Y. '60.

Lerner, Max. America as a civilization. Simon and Schuster. New York. '57.

Lipset, S. M. and Lowenthal, Leo, eds. Culture and social character: the work of David Riesman reviewed. Free Press. Glencoe, Ill. '61.

Longley, Marjorie and others, eds. America's taste; the cultural events of a century. Simon and Schuster. New York. '59.

Lowenthal, Leo. Literature, popular culture and society. Prentice-Hall. Englewood Cliffs, N.J. '61.

McCarthy, Mary. On the contrary. Farrar, Straus. New York. '61.

Macdonald, Dwight. Against the American grain. Random House. New York. '62.

Mannes, Marya. More in anger. Lippincott. Philadelphia. '58.

Montagu, Ashley. Cultured man. World. Cleveland. '58.

*Peyre, Henri. Observations on life, literature, and learning in America. Southern Illinois University Press. Carbondale. '61.

Phillips, William and Rahv, Philip, eds. Partisan Review anthology. Holt. New York. '62.

Read, Herbert. To hell with culture, and other essays on art and society. Schocken. New York. '63.

Riesman, David and others. Lonely crowd. Yale University Press. New Haven, Conn. '50.

Rosenberg, Bernard and White, D. M. Mass culture: the popular arts in America. Free Press. Glencoe, Ill. '57.

Rosenberg, Harold. Tradition of the new. Horizon. New York. '59.

Seldes, Gilbert. Public arts. Simon and Schuster. New York. '56.

Simonson, H. P. ed. Cross currents: a collection of essays from contemporary magazines. Harper. New York. '59.

Spiller, Robert and others, eds. American perspectives: the national self-image in the twentieth century. American Studies Association. Harvard University Press. Cambridge, Mass. '61.

Swados, Harvey. Radical's America. Little, Brown. Boston. '62.

Times (London). Literary Supplement. American imagination; a critical survey of the arts. Atheneum. New York. '60.

*United States. Senate. Arts and the national government; report to the President, May 28, 1963. August Heckscher. (Doc. no 28) 88th Congress, 1st session. Supt. of Docs. Washington 25, D.C. '63.

    Also reprinted in this book: Statement by President John F. Kennedy establishing the President's Advisory Council on the Arts, June 12, 1963. p 33-4.

Valentine, Alan. Age of conformity. Regnery. Chicago. '54.

Weales, Gerald. American drama since World War II. Harcourt. New York. '62.

Williams, Raymond. Long revolution. Columbia University Press. New York. '61.

PERIODICALS

ALA Bulletin. 56:716-20. S. '62. Libraries and the nation's cultural life. August Heckscher.

America. 103:491. Jl. 30, '60. Will culture survive?

America. 104:340-2. D. 3, '60. Culture explosion. C. J. McNaspy.

American Federationist. 69:9-12. Je. '62. Conserving America's cultural resources. H. D. Kenin.

*American Quarterly. 15:152-66. Sum. '63. Some observations on the concert audience. Stuart Levine.

American Scholar. 27:473-81. Fall '58. College students and reading. R. E. Ellsworth.

American Scholar. 28:61-71. Wint. '58-'59. Our serious comics. K. E. Eble.

American Scholar. 29:31-42. Wint. '59-'60. Quest of excellence: a humanistic utopia. Albert Guérard.

American Scholar. 29:55-72. Wint. '59-'60. Populist heritage and the intellectual. C. V. Woodward.

American Scholar. 29:201-8. Spr. '60. TV in the world of letters.

*American Scholar. 29:227-34. Spr. '60. Reflections on mass culture. Ernest van den Haag.

    Reply: 29:450+. Sum. '60. Gilbert Seldes.

Américas. 13:34-7. N. '61. Speaking of the United States: a survey of recent cultural trends. Jose Ferrater Mora.

Annals of the American Academy of Political and Social Science. 325:1-123. S. '59. American civilization and its leadership needs, 1960-1990; ed. by J. C. Charlesworth.

Antioch Review. 19:437-54. Wint. '59-'60. Quest for a new American culture. A. E. Meyer.

Antioch Review. 20:467-76. Wint. '60-'61. Arts today. Bertram Morris.

Atlantic. 209:131-4. Ap. '62. Money isn't everything. E. T. Chase.

*Business Week. p 36-8. D. 30, '61. Paperbacks: it pays to go highbrow.

Business Week. p 68-9. Ja. 19, '63. Arts become big business, too.

*College English. 23:417-36. Mr. '62. Mass culture/popular culture: notes for a humanist's primer. R. H. Pearce.

Columbia University Forum. 6:4-9. Sum. '63. Forms of plenty. J. M. Fitch.

Commentary. 31:160-6. F. '61. Sizing up the mass media. Harris Dienstfrey.

Commentary. 31:223-33. Mr. '61. Writing American fiction. Philip Roth.
    Discussion: 32:248-52. S. '61.

Commentary. 33:495-504. Je. '62. New American cinema. Harris Dienstfrey.
    Reply: 34:256-7. S. '62.

Commonweal. 70:247-50. Je. 5, '59. Culture critics. Walker Percy.

Commonweal. 74:445-7. Ag. 11, '61. Irrigating the TV wasteland. Nat Hentoff.

Commonweal. 75:271-4. D. 8, '61. Writer in America. J. P. Sisk.

Commonweal. 78:7-10. Mr. 29, '63. Mr. Minow's wasteland. Will Sparks.

Current History. 41:28-31+. Jl. '61. Higher education today. G. P. Burns.

*Daedalus. Spr. '60. Mass culture and mass media.
    Reprinted in this book: Parallel paths. Frank Stanton. p 347-53.

Daedalus. Wint. '63. American reading public.

Dance Magazine. 36:35-9+. Ja.; 34-5+. F. '62. At last Congress listens.

Dance Magazine. 36:48-51. Ap. '62. Community arts councils. Alvin Reiss.

Dun's Review & Modern Industry. 77:45-6+. My. '61. Booming market in mass culture. C. T. Slote.

Economist. 202:1255-6. Mr. 31, '62. Washington takes to the arts.

Film Quarterly. 12:23-31. Spr. '59. New Hollywood: myth and anti-myth. Robert Brustein.

*Fortune. 64:124-7+. N. '61. Quantity of culture. Alvin Toffler.

*Harper's Magazine. 219:173-9. O. '59. American poetry's silver age. Stanley Kunitz.

Harper's Magazine. 221:82-6+. Ag.; 85-90. S. '60. How good is TV at its best? Martin Mayer.

Harper's Magazine. 221:44-51. D. '60. Repertory fever. Robert Brustein.

Harper's Magazine. 224:31-9. Mr. '62 Contemporary art and the plight of its public. Leo Steinberg.

Horizon. 5:73-5. Ja. '63. Artist in our time. Murray Kempton.

Library Journal. 86:3223-8. O. 1, '61. Boom in books. P. J. Rosenwald.

Life. 47:62-3. D. 28, '59. Leisure could mean a better civilization.

Life. 49:44-5. D. 26, '60. In a second revolution, the new role for culture.

Life. 50:108-10+. My. 12, '61. No more a headache, book business booms. Ernest Havemann.

Life. 55:4-188. D. 20, '63. The movies. (Entire issue)

Look. 26:104-10. D. 18, '62. Arts in America; excerpt from Creative America. J. F. Kennedy.

Musical America. 79:22+. F. '59. Education must give high priority to the humanities. Howard Hanson.

Musical America. 82:9. Ag. '62. New frontiers: spread of musical culture. Everett Helm.

*Nation. 189:172-3. S. 26, '59. Show business is all business. Richard Hammer.

Nation. 191:454-7. D. 10, '60. Brain curtain: why America distrusts its intellectuals. Michael Novak.

Nation. 192:50-2. Ja. 21, '61. Lonely intellectual. Loren Baritz.

*Nation. 194:345-9. Ap. 21, '62. Pursuit of the real. F. R. Karl.

Nation. 194:350-4. Ap. 21, '62. Search for conflict. T. F. Driver.

Nation. 194:354-7. Ap. 21, '62. American finds his country. Hilton Kramer.

New Republic. 140:13-15. Mr. 30, '59. We don't know where we are: interview with Edmund Wilson; ed. by Henry Brandon.

New Republic. 144:10-12. Mr. 6, '61. More money, more learning? L. J. Hertzel.
   Discussion: 144:30-1. Mr. 13, '61.

New Republic. 144:20-2. My. 15, '61. How fair are the highbrows? John Cogley.

New Republic. 145:17. D. 11, '61. Who says we're soft? G. W. Johnson.

New Republic. 148:24-6. Ja. 26, '63. Continuing disaster. Paul Goodman.

New Republic. 148:8. Heckscher report. Je. 29, '63.

*New Statesman. 65:38. Ja. 11, '63. Culture machine. K. E. Meyer.
   Same abridged with title: Kulturvac 112 B: you can't lick it, it joins you. Newsweek. 61:26. Ja. 28, '63.

New York Times. Sec. II, p 7X. Jl. 31, '60. Background of National Cultural Center. Ross Parmenter.

New York Times. Sec. II, p 9X. O. 30, '60. Candidates on culture. H. C. Schonberg.

*New York Times. p 1+. N. 27, '61. Attendance soars at museums here. McCandlish Phillips.

New York Times. p 1. D. 15, '61. Goldberg urges U.S. to subsidize performing arts. Marjorie Hunter.

New York Times. p 40. D. 15, '61. Arts and the state. Howard Taubman.

New York Times. Sec. II, p 3X. D. 24, '61. Subsidy for the arts. Howard Taubman.

New York Times. Sec. II, p 9X. D. 31, '61. Arts hero, 1961. H. C. Schonberg.

New York Times. p 1+. F. 22, '62. White House names Heckscher to be coordinator of culture. Arthur Gelb.

New York Times. Sec. II, p 10X. Je. 3, '62. Art in a democracy. John Canaday.

*New York Times. Sec. II, p 4X. Je. 10, '62. Big count: half a million people engaged in non-utilitarian dance-watching. Allen Hughes.

New York Times. p 24. N. 21, '62. Culture running ahead of sports, study finds.

*New York Times. p 28. My. 24, '63. Merchandising of art is not really revolutionary. John Canaday.

*New York Times. p 22. Je. 17, '63. Cultural councils in thirteen states reflect an upsurge of interest. Milton Esterow.

*New York Times. p 44. S. 6, '63. Advertising: cultural magazines on plateau. Peter Bart.

*New York Times. p 87. O. 27, '63. Artist in America. J. F. Kennedy.

New York Times. p 1+. D. 16, '63. Ford fund allots 7.7 million to ballet. Allen Hughes.

New York Times. p 15. D. 30, '63. Johnson reviews cultural policy. Henry Raymont.

New York Times Book Review. p 68. N. 13, '60. 3d Annual Esquire Symposium. Writing in America today. Robert Gutwillig.
    Same with title: Dim views through fog. Esquire. 55:12+. F. '61.

New York Times Magazine. p 26+. O. 18, '59. Case against the tailfin age. E. D. Stone.
    Discussion: p 8+. N. 22, '59.

New York Times Magazine. p 14+. Jl. 9, '61. They're cultural, but are they cultured? Marya Mannes.

New York Times Magazine. p 14-15+. Ja. 14, '62. Reappraisal of the TV picture. Jack Gould.

*New York Times Magazine. p 26+. Mr. 11, '62. To come to the aid of the arts. A. J. Goldberg.

New York Times Magazine. p 18-19+. Jl. 29, '62. What, and who, sets the price of art? J. S. Held.

New York Times Magazine. pt 2. p 15+. S. 23, '62. Nation's culture: new age for the arts. August Heckscher.

New York Times Magazine. pt 2. p 17+. S. 23, '62. Music: we appreciate it, do we like it? Mark Schubart.

New York Times Magazine. p 22+. N. 4, '62. Not so popular as *Gunsmoke* but—. Richard Hoggart.

New York Times Magazine. p 21+. S. 22, '63. Have we 'culture'? yes—and no. William Schuman.

Newsweek. 59:102. My. 28, '62. Art-house boom.

Newsweek. 60:62. D. 3, '62. Culture business.

Newsweek. 60:23. D. 10, '62. Culture: a monstrous word.

Partisan Review. 19:282-326. My.-Je.; 420-50. Jl.-Ag.; 562-97. S.-O. '52. Our country and our culture: a symposium.

Partisan Review. 25:305-11+. Spr. '58. Know-nothing bohemians. Norman Podhoretz.
    Discussion: 25:472-9. Sum. '58.

Partisan Review. 26:560-72. Fall '59. Highbrows and the theater today. Louis Kronenberger.

Partisan Review. 26:593-605. Fall '59. Notes on a suburban theater. Robert Brustein.

Partisan Review. 26:107-16. Wint. '59. American establishment. William Phillips.

Partisan Review. 28:574-93. S./N. '61. Madison Avenue villain. Robert Brustein.

Partisan Review. 29:421-4. Sum. '62. Dupes of the art film. Penelope Gilliatt.

Public Opinion Quarterly. 26:377-88. Fall '62. On the use of the mass media as escape: clarification of a concept. Elihu Katz and David Foulkes.

Reader's Digest. 82:79-83. Ja. '63. Why Europeans criticize U.S.A. André Maurois.

Reporter. 21:43-4. Jl. 23, '59. What's wrong with culture? Alfred Kazin.

Reporter. 26:36-40. Mr. 29, '62. From Main Street to Madison Avenue. Louis Kronenberger.

Review of Politics. 21:389-401. Ap. '59. Contemporary art: generative role of play. J. J. Sweeney.

Saturday Evening Post. 234:26-7+. F. 25, '61. We're cultured too. J. A. Morris and R. P. Hanes, Jr.

Saturday Evening Post. 234:32-3+. Jl. 1, '61. Goal for Americans. H. M. Jones.

Saturday Evening Post. 234:19-25. O. 21; 56-8+. O. 28; 34+. N. 4; 62+. N. 11, '61. Television USA. J. B. Martin.

Saturday Evening Post. 235:12+. Mr. 24, '62. Speaking out: mental midgets take over. David Susskind.

Saturday Evening Post. 235:8+. Jl. 14, '62. Speaking out: who says I'm uncultured? Frederick Breitenfield, Jr.

Saturday Evening Post. 236:10+. Jl. 13, '63. Speaking out: national "culture explosion" is phony. H. C. Schonberg.

Saturday Review. 43:15-17+. Mr. 12, '60. Can modern art survive its friends? Katharine Kuh.

Saturday Review. 43:80-1. Mr. 12, '60. Medici for our time. Oliver Daniel.

Saturday Review. 43:11-13+. Je. 18, '60. Individual in a mass culture. George Gerbner.

Saturday Review. 43:11-13+. Ag. 6, '60. No hix in the stix? D. W. Brogan.

Saturday Review. 43:16. Ag. 13, '60. Highbrow and the Midcult. Granville Hicks.

Saturday Review. 43:43-53. D. 24, '60. Are foreign films better? symposium.

*Saturday Review. 44:21-3+. F. 25, '61. Growing pains of a shrinking industry. Arthur Mayer.

Saturday Review. 44:11-13. Mr. 18, '61. Who reads the classics? H. C. Webster.

Saturday Review. 44:50-1+. N. 18, '61. What college students read. F. D. Bolman and Eugene Arden.

Saturday Review. 44:32+. D. 23, '61. New frontier in art? Katharine Kuh.

Saturday Review. 44:33, 34-6. D. 23, '61. Shop talk in Hollywood: panel discussion; ed. by Arthur Knight.

*Saturday Review. 45:30A-30P. S. 8, '62. Art in America in 1962. Katharine Kuh.

Saturday Review. 45:11-12. D. 29, '62. Studios without walls. Arthur Knight.

Saturday Review. 46:15-16. F. 9, '63. What's missing in the novel? Leonore Marshall.

*Saturday Review. 46:61+. Ap. 13, '63. Newspapers and the culture beat. John Tebbel.

School and Society. 90:5-21. Ja. 13, '62; 91:5-21. Ja. 12, '63. Statistics of attendance in American universities and colleges 1961-1963.

Senior Scholastic. 76:38-9. My. 4, '60. America's musical renaissance. Roy Hemming.

Senior Scholastic. 77:10-11. N. 30, '60. America: cultural wonderland or wasteland? William Lineberry.

Spectator. 205:591+. O. 21, '60. Those egg-head blues. Peter Michaels.

Spectator. 209:502-4. O. 5, '62. Other end of the dumb-bell. Thomas Griffith.

*Theatre Arts. 45:25-6+. My. '61. Theatre across the country. Alan Pryce-Jones.

Theatre Arts. 45:8-10+. Je. '61. There's nothing wrong with movies. Arthur Knight.

Theatre Arts. 45:62-5+. S. '61. Dance finds roots of grass. Doris Her-
ing.

Time. 76:70-2. Ag. 22, '60. Era of non-B.

Time. 79:56+. My. 25, '62. Rise of mass culture.

U.S. News & World Report. 54:68-72. Ap. 8, '63. Culture: getting to be
big business.

Virginia Quarterly Review. 35:627-34. Fall '59. Humanizing our dangerous age. W. R. Agard.

*Vital Speeches of the Day. 27:533-7. Je. 15, '61. Program control:
broadcasters are public trustees. N. N. Minow.

Vital Speeches of the Day. 27:568-71. Jl. 1, '61. Television and the
pursuit of excellence. Louis Hausman.

Vital Speeches of the Day. 29:205-9. Ja. 15, '63. Intellectual and the
market place. G. J. Stigler.

Vogue. 141:136-9. F. 1, '63. Not sealed off from life. Louis Kronenberger.

Wilson Library Bulletin. 36:238-41. N. '61. Reading of today's college
students. Joseph Mersand.

Wilson Library Bulletin. 36:274+. D. '61. Paperback explosion.

Yale Review. 50:219-25. D. '60. Arts, the sciences, and scholarship.
J. S. Fruton.

Yale Review. 51:593-608. Je. '62. Hollywood faces the world. R. D.
MacCann.